Space Science

44 ACTIVITIES, EXPERIMENTS, AND PROJECTS

Ormiston H. Walker

illustrated by Loyd Birmingham

J. WESTON
WALCH
PUBLISHER
Portland, Maine

User's Guide
to
Walch Reproducible Books

As part of our general effort to provide educational materials which are as practical and economical as possible, we have designated this publication a "reproducible book." The designation means that purchase of the book includes purchase of the right to limited reproduction of all pages on which this symbol appears:

Here is the basic Walch policy: We grant to individual purchasers of this book the right to make sufficient copies of reproducible pages for use by all students of a single teacher. This permission is limited to a single teacher, and does not apply to entire schools or school systems, so institutions purchasing the book should pass the permission on to a single teacher. Copying of the book or its parts for resale is prohibited.

Any questions regarding this policy or requests to purchase further reproduction rights should be addressed to:

Permissions Editor
J. Weston Walch, Publisher
321 Valley Street • P. O. Box 658
Portland, Maine 04104-0658

Photo Credits

Photos 1, 2, 4–6, 9, 11–14: NASA (National Aeronautics and Space Administration)

Photo 3: National Climatic Data Center

Photos 7, 8, 10: ©1994 Digital Stock Inc.

---

1   2   3   4   5   6   7   8   9   10

ISBN 0-8251-02856-0

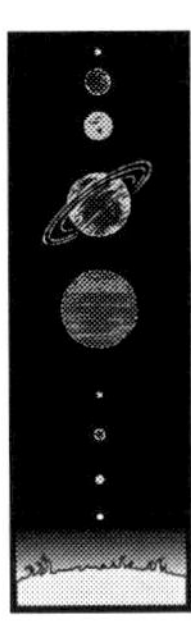

CONTENTS

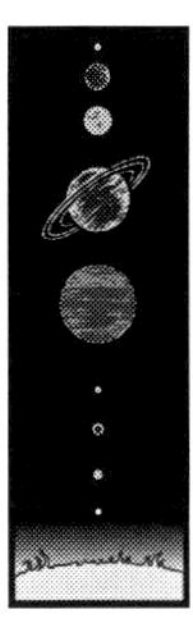

INTRODUCTION

Space Science: 44 Activities, Experiments, and Projects is a companion volume for *Astronomical! 44 Activities, Experiments, and Projects,* also published by J. Weston Walch, Publisher. It provides resources for study of four major topics connected with space exploration:

The physics of space flight
Space vehicles
Probing the cosmos
Humans in space

The activities and demonstrations in this book can be done in a classroom setting during the day with readily available materials. A few of the activities call for reagents, such as hydrochloric acid, found in most high school chemistry laboratories. All usual safety precautions must be employed while students participate in these activities.

This classroom resource also features five activities with reproducible pages:

- Model flight paths using conic sections: pages 25–27

- Show how to calculate the distance above the earth a satellite must orbit in order to be "geosynchronous": page 32

- Make an autogyro to demonstrate spacecraft soft landings: page 45

- Show topological concepts underlying spacecraft design by making a Möbius strip: page 48

- Investigate the structure of crystals that form nearly perfectly in space: pages 65–68

With this book, and your imagination, you will learn how human beings have overcome the significant obstacles of gravity and atmosphere in order to take small steps beyond our earth. Perhaps one day you will be an observer or explorer of the faraway worlds that await our arrival

CHAPTER ONE

THE PHYSICS OF SPACE FLIGHT

1. Earth's Gravity

Whence arises all that order and beauty we see in the world?

—Sir Isaac Newton

We make use of gravity when we weigh something, for weight is the result of the earth's gravity pull. Gravity holds satellites in orbit around the earth; it also keeps the planets moving harmoniously in their orbits around the sun. Ever since the days of Galileo, humans have been interested in the nature of gravity—the mysterious force that attracts objects to the center of the earth. It is as formidable as it is mysterious, requiring us to build immensely powerful machines in order to lift objects into orbit.

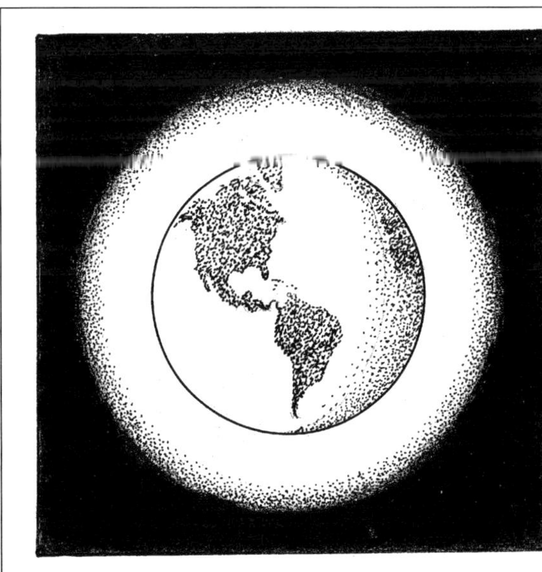

Figure 1-1.
The earth's
atmosphere is
held in place
by the pull of
gravity.

The earth is not a perfect sphere. It bulges at the equator and is flattened at the poles. As a result, gravity varies from place to place over the globe. It also varies with height above sea level and with the heaviness or lightness of minerals within the earth's crust.

Sir Isaac Newton developed the Law of Universal Gravitation. This law tells us that all masses attract each other with a force proportional to the product of their masses and inversely proportional to the square of their distance apart.

Measurements of gravity are made by recording the time a pendulum takes to swing through its arc. The method is exact. But it is very slow, as a great many swings are necessary. So scientists use a gravity meter, which is a very sensitive spring scale. Gravity meters measure the difference in pull in relation to your distance from the center of the earth. But gravity also depends on the mass of a body. Over a lightweight area in the earth's crust, the gravity meter gives a lower reading than over very dense areas. Using this principle, oil companies look for petroleum in the earth's crust. Deposits of metal ores may be located in the same way.

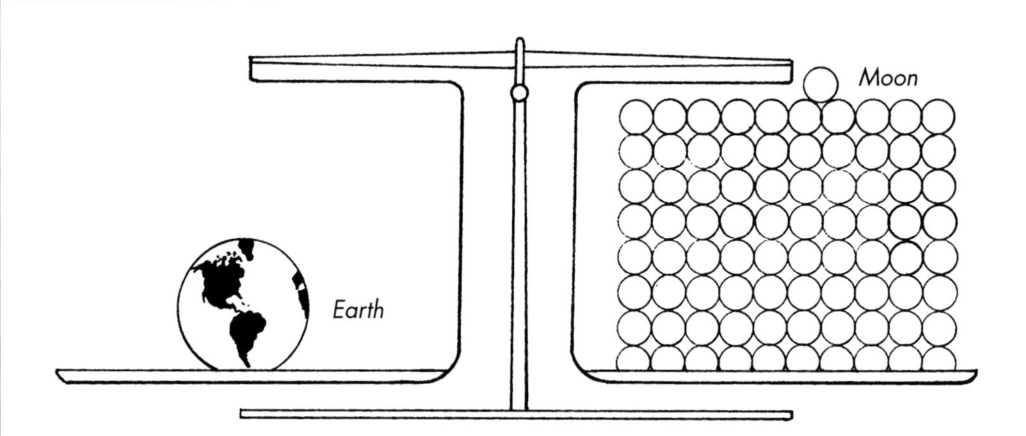

Figure 1-2. The beam balance compares masses. Mass is the amount of matter in an object. Mass is a fundamental quantity. Weight is the pull of gravity on it. Weight is a force. It is proportional to an object's mass and inversely proportional to the square of the distance between the object and center of the earth (or other body).

The gravitational pull of the earth is large because of its large mass, 5.98×10^{24} kg. The moon, having a much smaller mass, 7.35×10^{22} kg, has a smaller gravitational pull. The mass of the earth is close to 81 times that of the moon (Figure 1-2).

The Nature of Gravity

You may carry out some experiments on the nature of gravity.

What you need: weight, elastic, electric fan, air-filled balloon, different-sized marbles or other objects, drinking straw, glass of drinking water, blotting or filter paper, container of ink or colored water, white flower on its stem, helium balloon, block of wood, basin of water, bar magnets, copper nails, book, 10×15-cm baseboard, paper bag, rubber tubing, two glasses of plain water

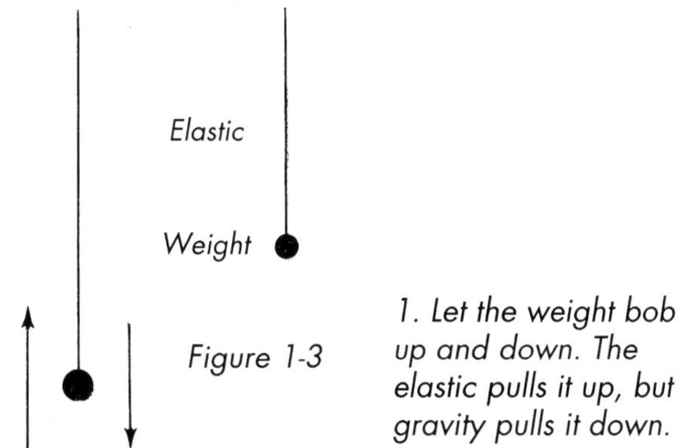

Figure 1-3

1. Let the weight bob up and down. The elastic pulls it up, but gravity pulls it down.

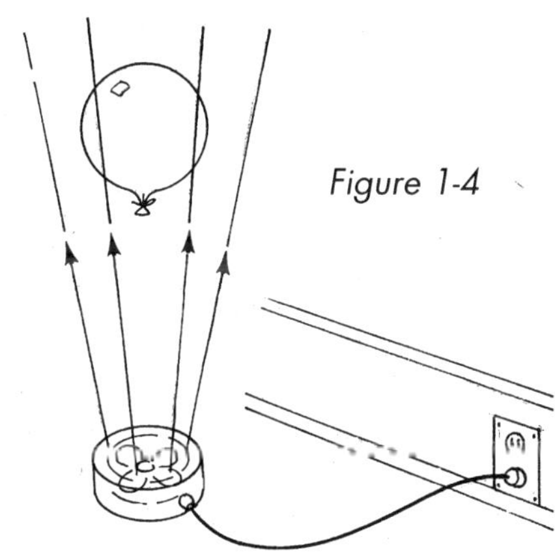

Figure 1-4

2. The upward push of air on the balloon works against the downward pull of gravity.

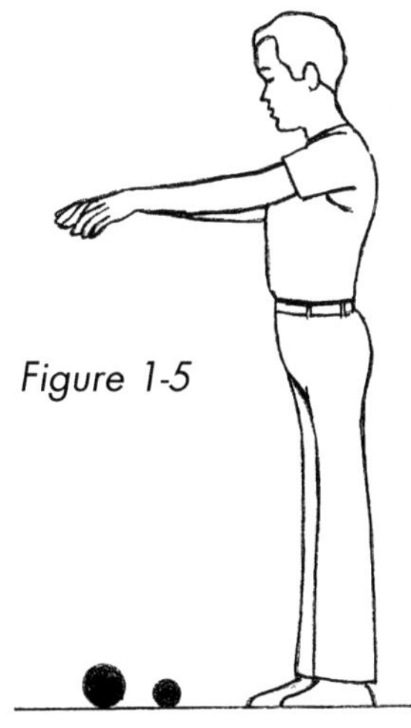

Figure 1-5

3. Let the different-sized marbles (or other objects) drop simultaneously. How do they reach the ground? What can you say about the pull of gravity on objects of different dimensions and weights?

Figure 1-6

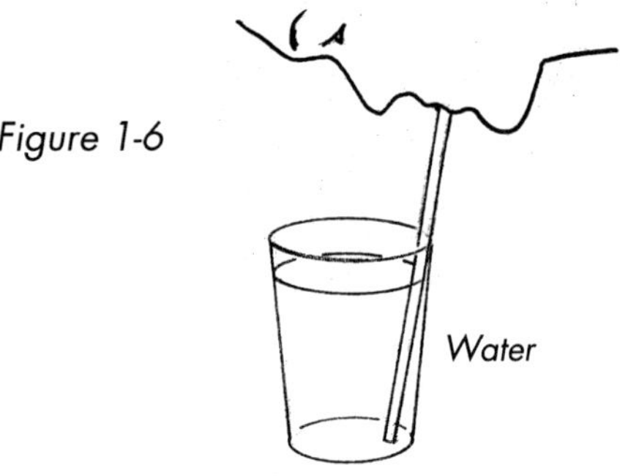

4. Suck water through the drinking straw. Explain how the pull of gravity is overcome.

Figure 1-7

5. Dip the piece of blotting paper or filter paper in the ink or colored water. What happens? What can you say about capillarity vs. gravity?

Figure 1-8

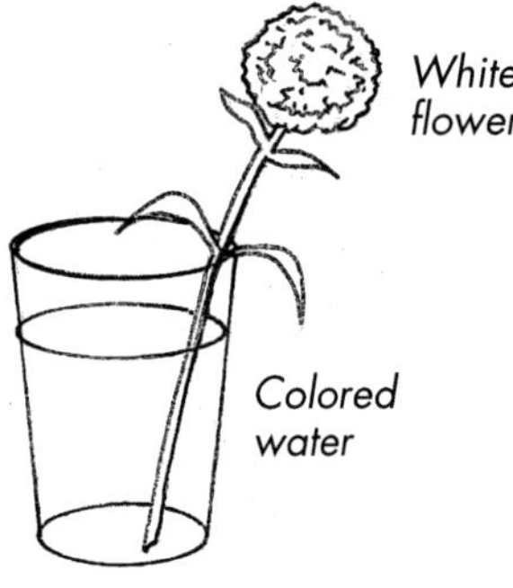

6. Place a white flower — a white carnation works well— in a glass of water containing red dye. What do you notice about the flower in the morning? How has gravity been overcome?

Figure 1-9

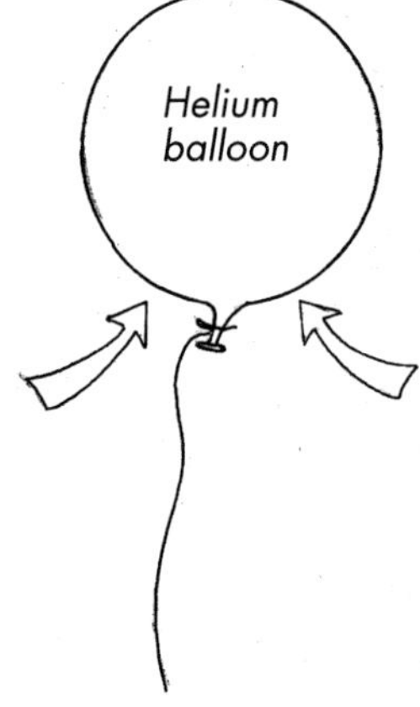

7. Explain why the helium balloon floats. How is air pressure helping to overcome gravity?

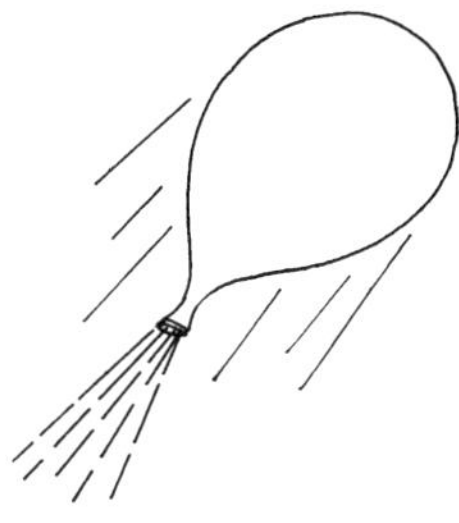

8. Release the inflated balloon. Explain the rocket action of the balloon. What overcomes gravity?

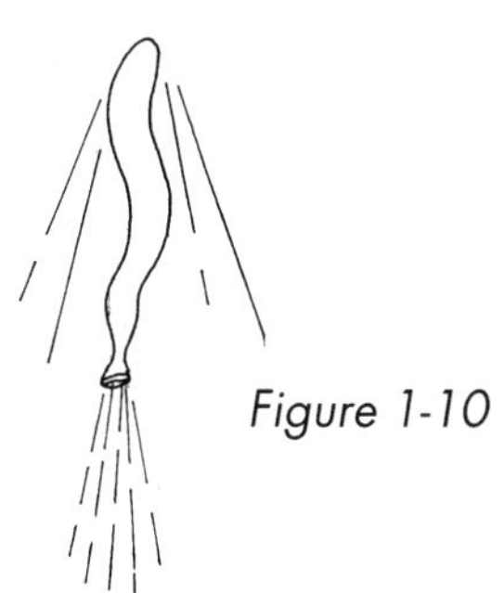

Figure 1-10

Figure 1-11

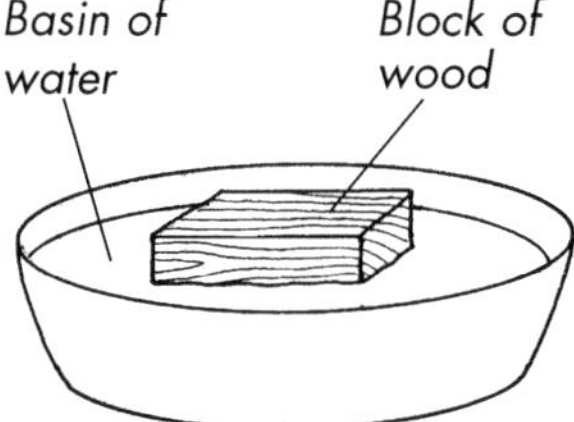

9. Place the block of wood in the water. What buoys it? Explain how gravity is balanced.

Figure 1-12

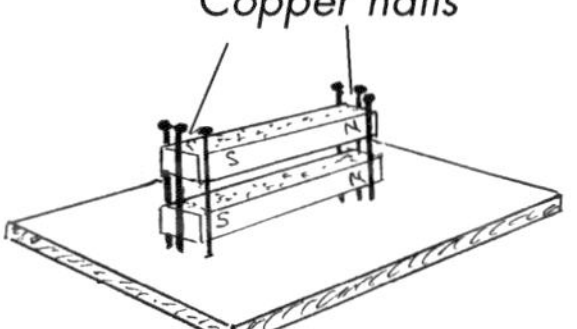

10. Set up the magnets as shown. Explain how magnetic force and gravity are at work.

Figure 1-13

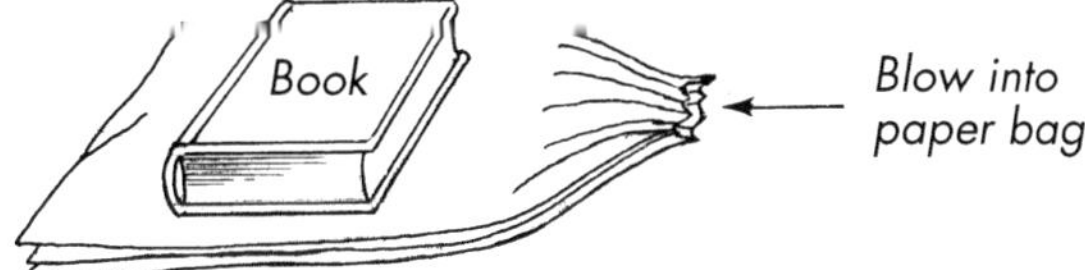

11. Place the book on the empty paper bag, then blow into the bag. How are gravity and air pressure both at work?

Figure 1-14

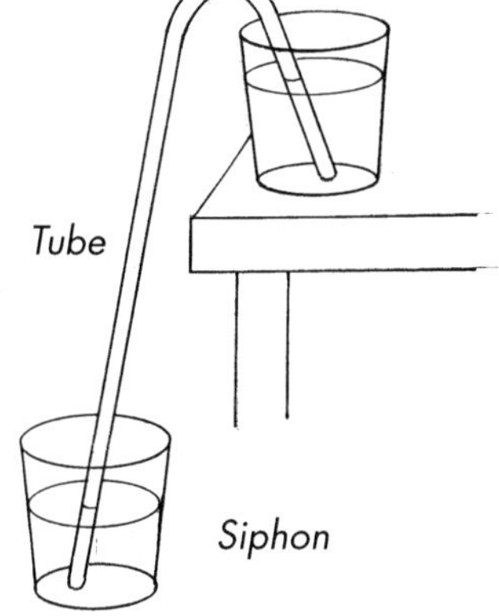

12. Set up a siphon as shown. Suck at the lower end to get the siphon working. Explain how water is able to flow uphill against the downward pull of gravity.

2. Motion

Sir Isaac Newton published three laws of motion in 1686. All objects in motion obey these laws. By applying them, we are able to send spacecraft to the moon and put satellites in orbit around the earth.

In the first law of motion, Newton said that a body at rest tends to stay at rest and a body in motion tends to stay in motion at constant speed in a straight line, unless some outside force acts on it. A force from outside may be muscle, gravity, or forces of magnetism or electricity. When you lift a book, you use muscle force. A magnet attracts an iron nail by magnetic force. A tennis ball on your table is at rest because the upward push of the table balances the downward pull of gravity. The side forces* acting on it also help balance it. Therefore, the tennis ball is stationary. If you apply muscle force to it, the forces acting on the ball no longer balance and motion will occur. But the tennis ball will not move of its own accord.

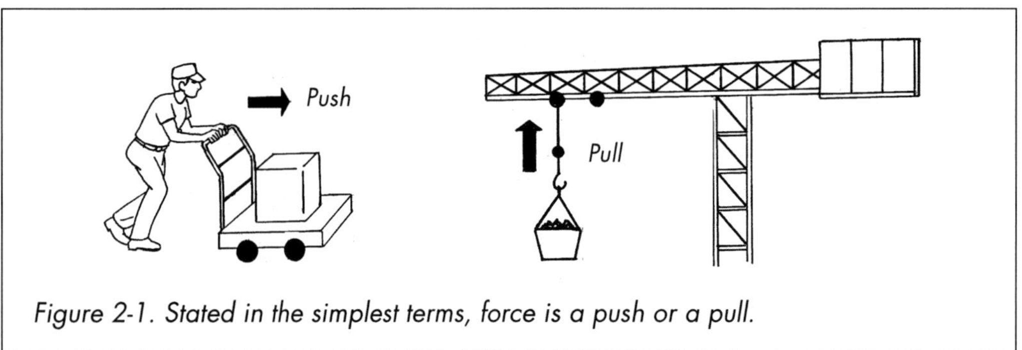

Figure 2-1. Stated in the simplest terms, force is a push or a pull.

The second law of motion tells us that an object accelerates (speeds up) in proportion to the force applied to it. When you press on the accelerator in a car, the engine revs up and develops more push, and the car speeds up. But if you fill up the car with people, making it heavier, you will need more force to speed it up. For example, if the mass is doubled, the acceleration is halved. If the weight is four times as great, the acceleration is reduced to one quarter, and so on, for a constant force.

Observing Motion

In the activities described on the next page, you can observe how objects behave when set in motion and relate their movement to Newton's first two laws of motion. For the third law, see page 9, "Thrust at Liftoff."

---

* the hammering of air particles all over the ball

What you need: cardboard box with lid, coin, card, plasticene, marble, string, glass

First law

1. Place your box on a table. Push it, then pull it. Push and pull are forces. The forces are external—they are due to an outside factor or agent, your hand. Which part of Newton's first law of motion have you demonstrated? (Figure 2-2.)

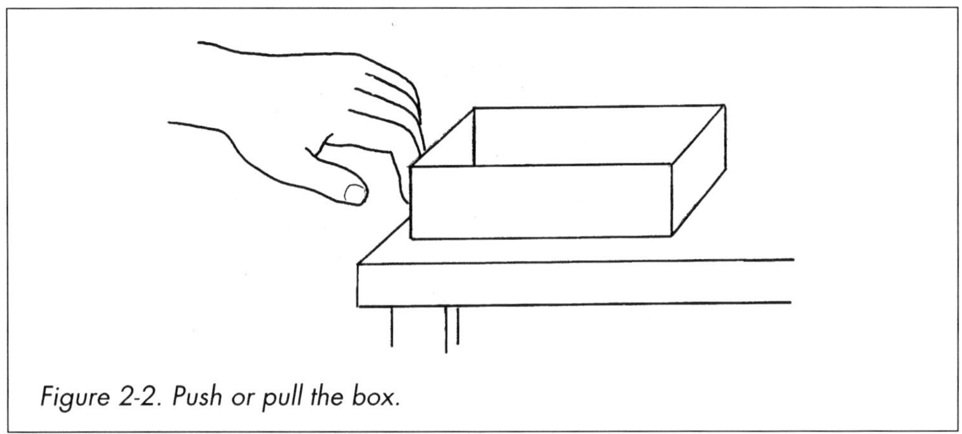

Figure 2-2. Push or pull the box.

2. Push the marble lightly on a smooth, polished surface. Does it travel in a straight line, at a constant rate—for the start, anyway? What force slows the marble down, bringing it finally to rest (Figure 2-3)?

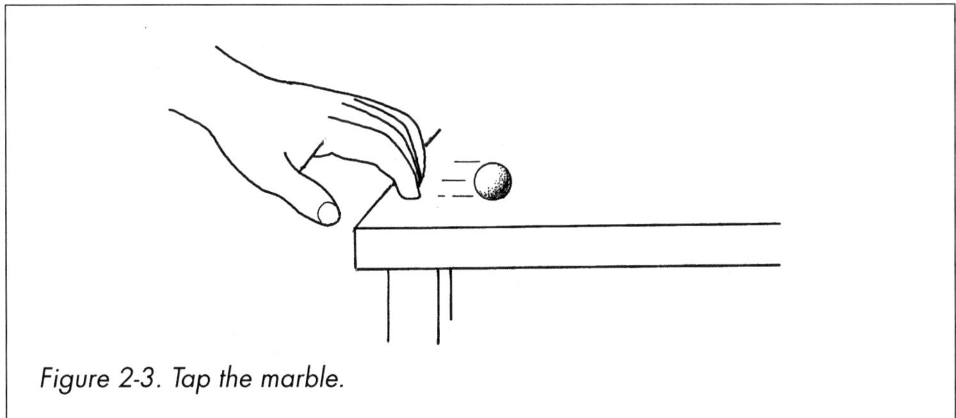

Figure 2-3. Tap the marble.

Push the marble so that it rolls along the table and over the edge. Does the marble change direction? What part of the first law have you demonstrated? What force acts to cause the change of direction (Figure 2-4)?

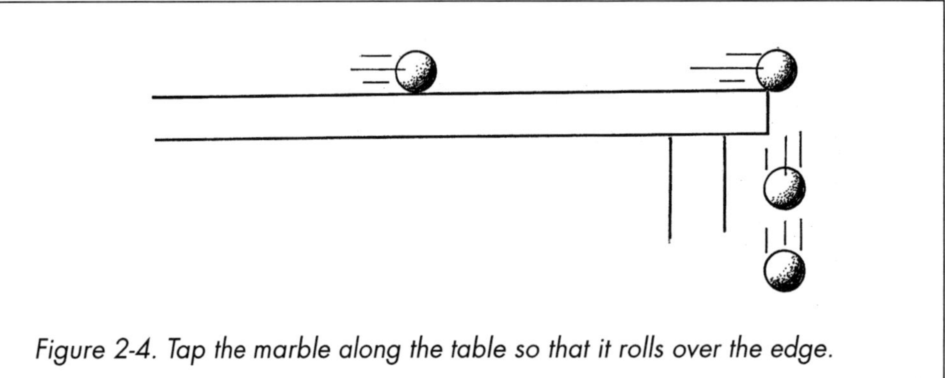

Figure 2-4. Tap the marble along the table so that it rolls over the edge.

Friction

3. Place the box on a smooth surface and give it a sharp push. Note how far it travels. Repeat this on the carpet or on a rug. What difference do you find? Can you explain why? When one body moves over another, roughnesses in the surfaces tend to get caught up in one another. The rougher the surfaces, the greater the frictional force opposing motion. Since no surface is absolutely smooth, friction cannot be completely avoided.

4. Roll the marble across the floor, then push the box. Which travels farther? How do the motions compare? Explain how frictional forces help the marble roll. How does friction act differently on the sliding box? What frictional force acts on a rocket rising above earth? How does shape help to lessen friction?

Inertia

5. Place the box on a sheet of paper. Pull the paper gently. What happens? Then, with a quick jerk, pull the paper away. What happens to the box? Because of inertia, the box resists any change in motion and so stays where it is. What about the force of friction between the paper and the box? Why is a sharp pull required to pull the paper away?

Second law

6. Using a smooth surface, give the marble a gentle tap (force). Does the marble accelerate? Along what kind of path? Repeat, giving the marble a harder tap. Does the marble travel faster? With greater force, what can you say about the acceleration? To accelerate a car, what must the driver do to make the engine supply increased force? To decelerate the car, what must the driver do? How is a space capsule returning to earth decelerated?

3. Thrust at Liftoff

Whenever body A exerts a force on body B, body B exerts on body A a force that is equal in magnitude, but opposite in direction. This is Newton's third law of motion. Usually one force is called the action, and the other, the reaction. The law is usually stated like this: For every action, there is an equal and opposite reaction (Figure 3-1).

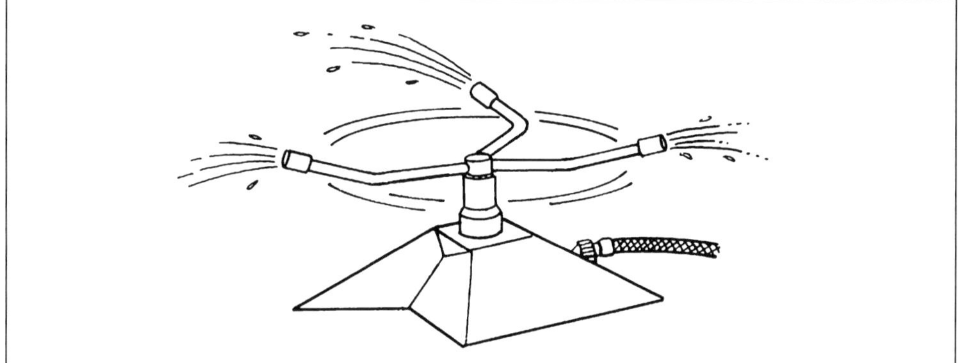

Figure 3-1. Action-reaction lawn sprinkler. The action of the water spurting out of the jets produces the reaction that spins the sprinkler.

When you jump, you push against the ground and the ground pushes back on you with equal force. A rock on the ground experiences the downward pull of gravity (action). The rock's gravity exerts an upward pull on the earth (reaction).

The forward movement of a rocket or jet-propelled aircraft results from the backward force or thrust of hot gases under pressure exiting the exhausts (Figure 3-2).

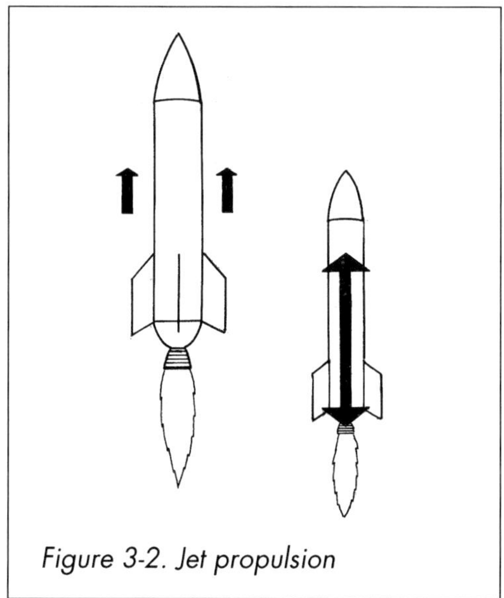

Figure 3-2. Jet propulsion

The action-reaction principle is also seen in everyday things such as roller-skating, rowing, and the kickback of a gun when it is fired. Thrust is also shown when a balloon streaks away from you as the gases gush out of its nozzle. In rockets and all aircraft, the principle is in continuous operation.

Photo 1. The space shuttle Discovery *lifts off from its launch pad at the Kennedy Space Center in Florida on July 13, 1995, for a 7-day, 22-hour flight.*

Newton's Third Law in Action

What you need: balloons—round and sausage-shaped, sand, paper cup, nail, candle, matches, thread, water, two 3-cm pieces of drinking straw, stone, rubber band, board, two round pencils, cardboard carton, cardboard, scissors, plasticene, plastic pen cap, needle

1. Blow up the round balloon and release the nozzle against a small pile of sand. What happens to the pile of sand? Repeat, but this time try squeezing the balloon. What happens to the pile of sand this time (Figure 3-3)?

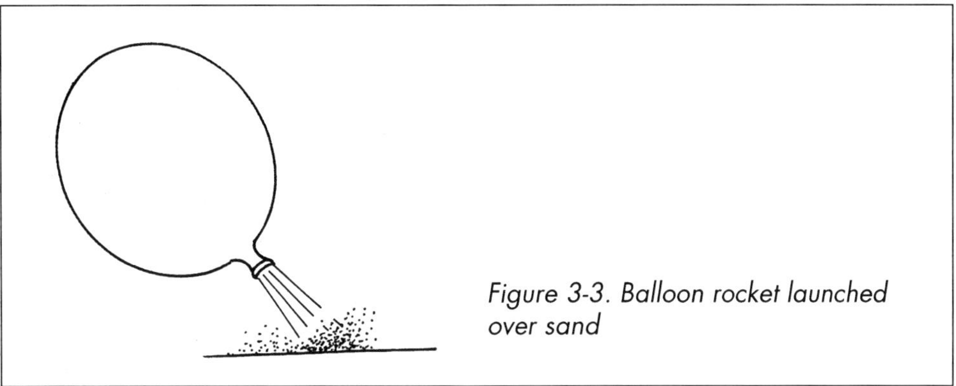

Figure 3-3. Balloon rocket launched over sand

2. Blow up the round balloon again, release the nozzle, and let the balloon go. Describe what happens. Does the balloon streak away from you? How is the balloon acting as a rocket? What are the forces of action and reaction (Figure 3-4)?

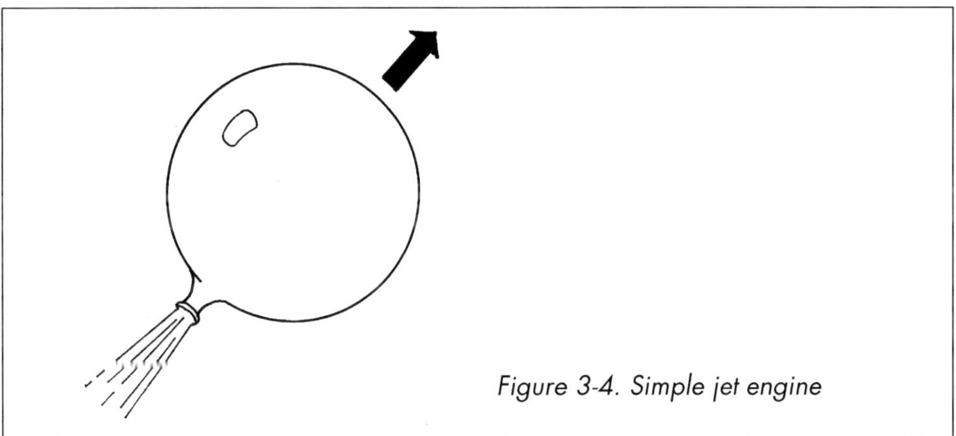

Figure 3-4. Simple jet engine

3. Use a nail to make two 2–3 mm holes opposite each other at the base of the paper cup. Place a 3-cm-long piece of drinking straw in each of the holes, parallel to each other, with open ends pointing in opposite directions. Seal these in position with candle wax, but do not block the straws (Figure 3-5).

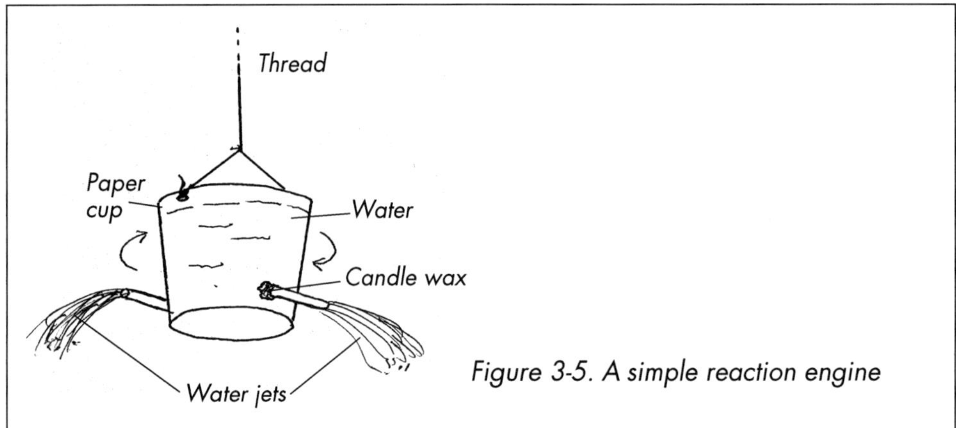

Figure 3-5. A simple reaction engine

Suspend the paper cup with thread as shown in the diagram; fill it with water. Describe what happens. The device you have made is called a reaction engine. What does this mean?

4. Place the stone on the board, which rests on two round pencils as shown. Tie the band to the nail with a short piece of string so that the band is under tension. Use a match to burn through the string, releasing the tension. How does the board move? How about the stone? How does this show Newton's law of action-reaction? Experiment with stones of different sizes, and different tensions in the rubber band (Figure 3-6).

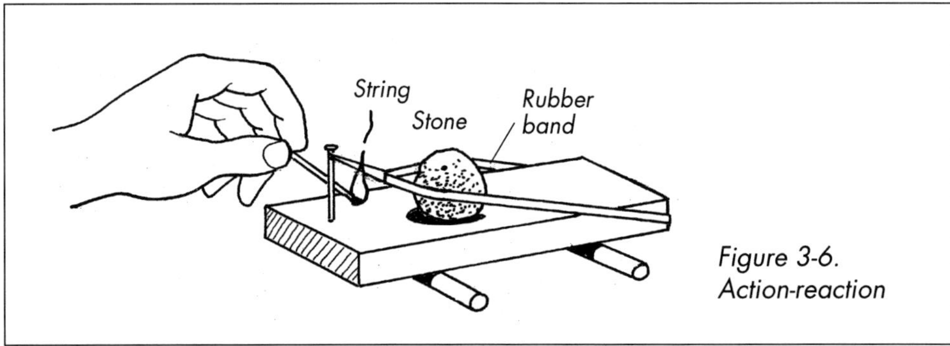

Figure 3-6. Action-reaction

5. Jet propulsion—model rocket ship. Make a model rocket ship from cardboard and other materials as shown in Figure 3-7. Experiment with a sausage-shaped balloon; blow it up and place it in the cardboard cradle, then release it. In which direction does the rocket ship move as compared with the direction of the escaping air? Experiment with thread to vary the size of the balloon nozzle. When does the air escape most freely? When does your rocket ship travel faster?

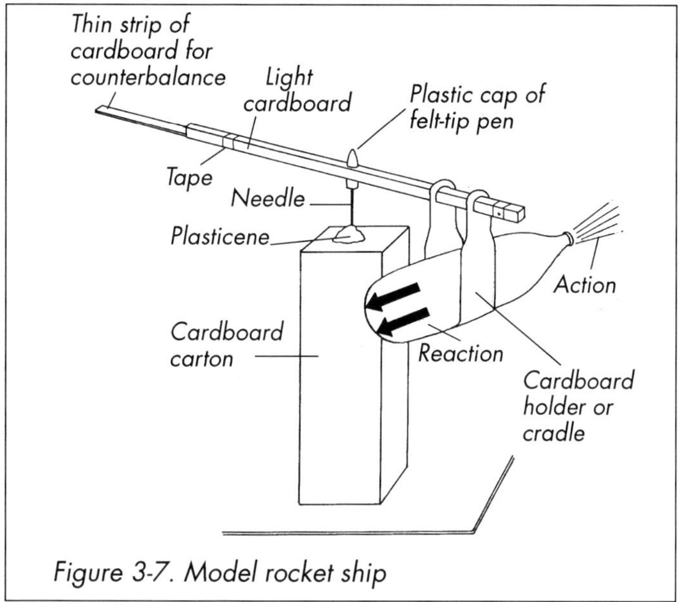

Figure 3-7. Model rocket ship

4. Weightless Liquids

Liquid fuels used in rockets are transferred from rocket storage tanks by a method that uses small pumps and pressurized gas. This method works well while the rocket is on the launching pad or in powered flight. Scientists found that when a spacecraft was orbiting, however, it was more difficult.

When liquids are free of the earth's gravity, the cohesive forces between the molecules in the surface of the liquid pull it into sphere-shaped globules. Vibration of the spacecraft caused these globules to float around the storage tanks so that the pump-gas method no longer worked.

One method used to overcome this (called the "posigrade" method) is to fire small rockets. This gives the spacecraft a slight acceleration, making the fuel pile up at the combustion end of the tanks. Another method uses a collapsible plastic bag to contain the fuel; this continually presses the fuel toward the pumps, not allowing it to break up into droplets.

Observing a Weightless Liquid

You can see how the behavior of a liquid changes in the weightless state.

What you need: clear plastic tubing (Lucite™ or other plastic, 75 cm long, diameter about 2 cm), corks for the ends, water, food coloring, video camera (optional)

1. Cork one end of the tube, then fill with colored water to within 7–8 cm of the top. Finally, cork the other end. Tape securely.

2. Turn the tube upside down and note what happens. Can you explain why the air bubble rises to the top?

3. Now invert the tube again. Immediately toss it 2-3 meters through the air to a friend. Watch the air bubble closely during flight, when the tube is falling freely. What happens to the air bubble during flight? When does the bubble rise to the top this time? Can you explain its behavior as compared with Step 2 above?

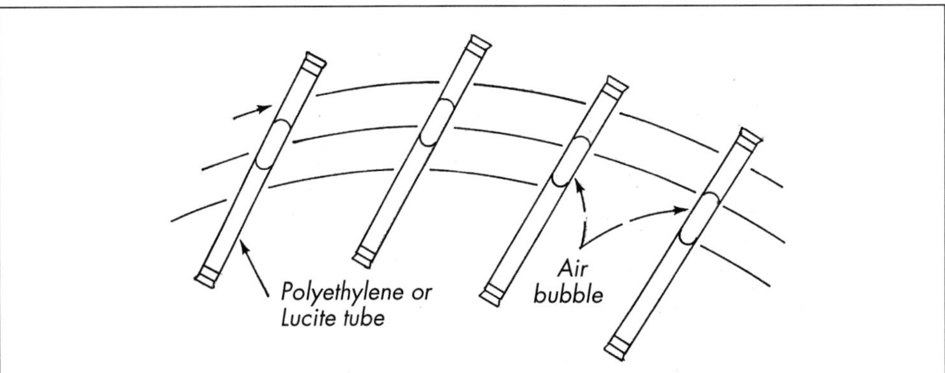

Figure 4-1. Use clear plastic tubing filled with water and corked at both ends to demonstrate the behavior of an air bubble during flight.

4. If possible, take the tube upstairs, invert it as before, then let it fall to a friend below. Again, observe the behavior of the air bubble. Why does free-fall affect its behavior? Is gravity absent? What did Einstein say about gravity and free-fall?

5. (optional) If you have a video camera and videotape player with slow-motion control, try filming the tube during flight, then play it back in slow motion. Write about your observations.

6. When the tube is inverted and the bubble rises, what scientific principle is involved? Who discovered it? Write a paragraph describing the discovery.

5. Streamlines—Finding the Best Shape

> *Tugged till the toadstool*
> *Toppled in two.*
> *Holding it over him,*
> *Gaily he flew,*
>
> —Oliver Herford, *"The Elf and the Dormouse"*

Shape has a strong effect on the frictional forces opposing an object's movement through fluid media like air and water. A flat disc or square of cardboard, like a flying wing, a rocket, a spacecraft, a skimming stone, a boomerang, or a dart, moves through the air easily.

When you flick a playing card, you give it spinning energy that helps it to slice through the air with very little resistance to its motion. That's because of its shape. A tapering cigar-shaped piece of plasticene reaches the bottom of a jar of water ahead of a flat plasticene disc, showing clearly how shape helps the flow of fluid—water or air— over it. Three different shapes made from soft wood, whether you throw them as far as possible, drop them from a height, or pull them through water with a string, also show there is a best shape for motion.

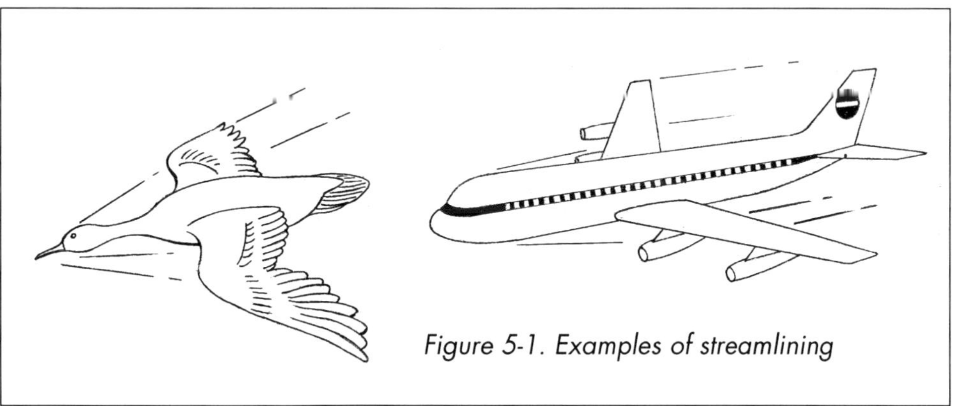

Figure 5-1. Examples of streamlining

The smoothing and polishing of surfaces is important also. The smoothing of rivets and polishing of an aircraft's wings can add up to 25 kilometers per hour to its speed. On the other hand, many spacecraft are designed with blunt noses so they can use the earth's atmosphere to cushion reentry.

Exploring Streamlined Shapes

You can find the shape that best helps the force producing motion.

What you need: a playing card or similar piece of cardboard, shapes made from soft wood, balsa wood or a stick, workshop tools, dowels, light cardboard, plasticene, two jars of water

1. Try throwing the playing card flat into the air; notice how far it travels. Now place the card on the edge of a book and tap the free end. How far does it travel this time? How does shape—spin—help (Figure 5-2)?

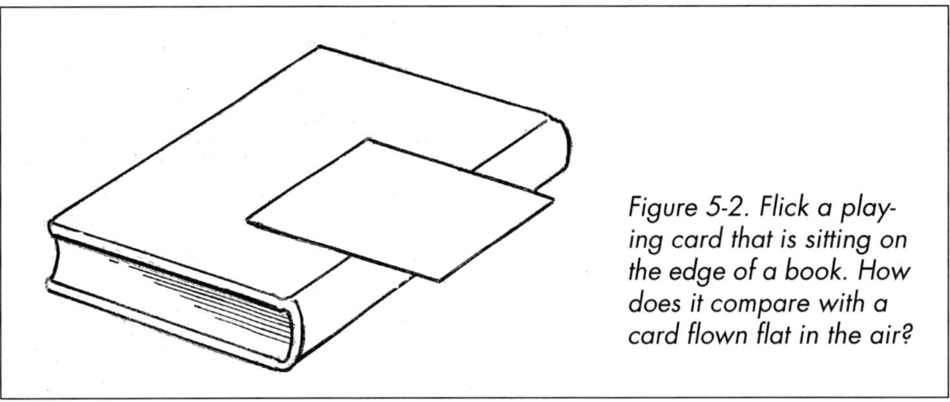

Figure 5-2. Flick a playing card that is sitting on the edge of a book. How does it compare with a card flown flat in the air?

2. Dip your hand into a jar of water and let some drops fall against light from a window. Note the shape the drops take. Sketch some. How does their shape help them in moving (Figure 5-3)?

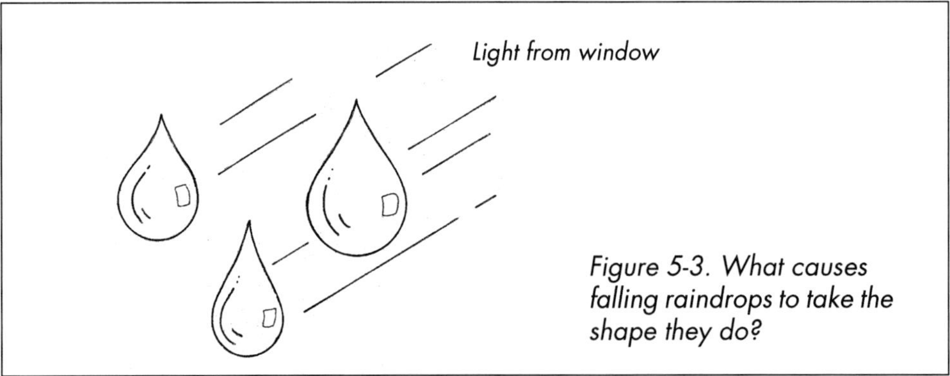

Figure 5-3. What causes falling raindrops to take the shape they do?

3. Have a handy person in your class make the shapes in Figure 5-4. Go outside to a safe area and throw them as far as possible many times until you see the average throw for each type. Measure the distance each type travels. Which shape travels the farthest? Which shape is best for travel? Try to draw the streamlines, showing how the air flows around each shape.

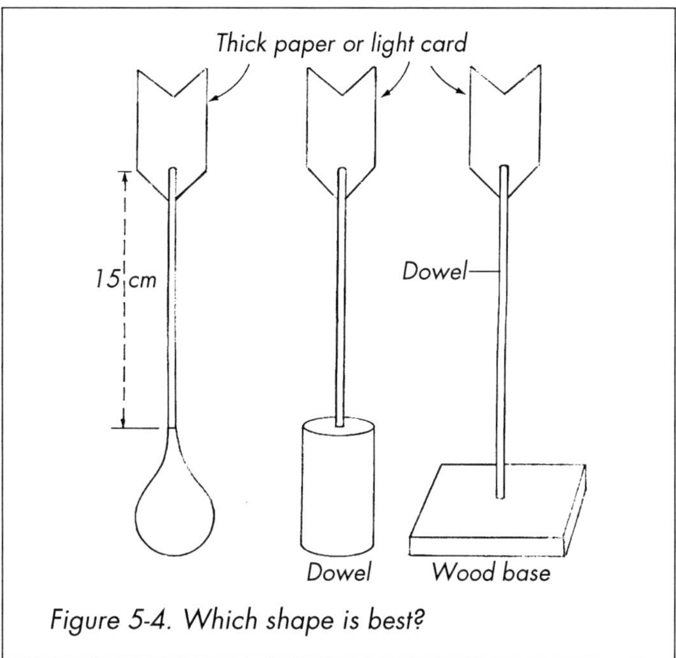

Figure 5-4. Which shape is best?

4. Take two pieces of plasticene the same size. Press one into a smooth, flat disc about 5 cm across. Make the other into a tapering cigar shape. Drop the flat disc into one jar of water and the cigar shape into the other, releasing each at the same instant (Figure 5-5). Which shape reaches the bottom of the jar first? Explain why. How does shape affect movement? Which shape is best?

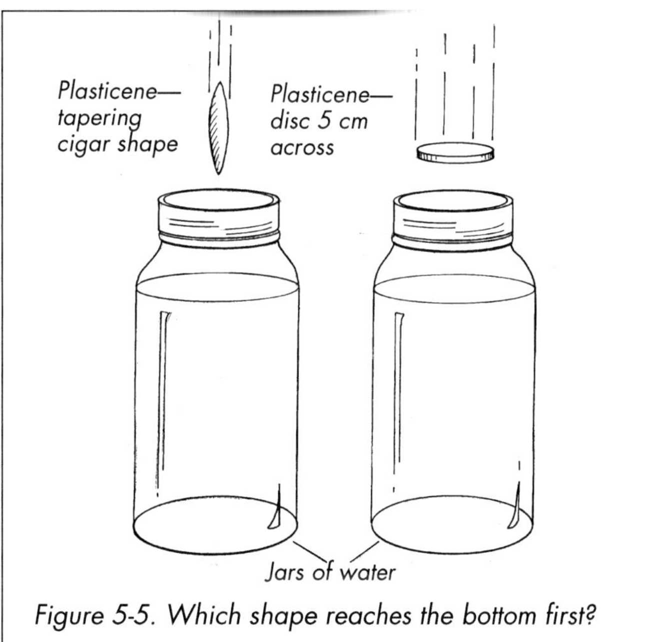

Figure 5-5. Which shape reaches the bottom first?

6. Stability and Control

Lift and propulsion both depend on a smooth, even flow of air over the wing and body surface. This is the reason for streamlining. Birds and the space shuttle are alike because they are highly streamlined; so also are fish, boats, and water insects. A blunt torpedo shape is most effective in producing this even flow and in avoiding air resistance. A bird's body, a wing in cross-section, and the back swimmer (a pond insect) all use this basic streamlined shape.

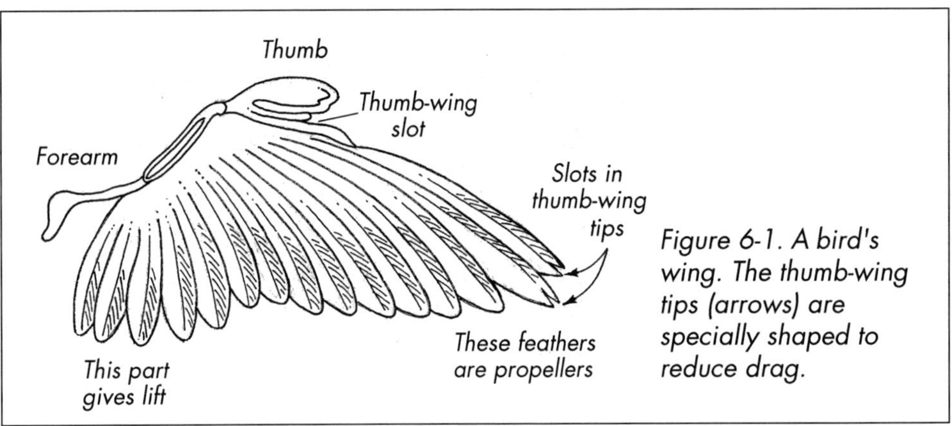

Figure 6-1. A bird's wing. The thumb-wing tips (arrows) are specially shaped to reduce drag.

If streamlining is lacking, or if flight is too slow, eddy currents are produced, particularly at the wing tips and in the wake. These produce drag and cause stalling. Birds and some aircraft have special devices to avoid this. Some aircraft have slots on the leading margin of the wing. These open at low speeds to spill air through onto the upper wing surface and so wash away eddies. The thumb-wing in birds, which opens from the main wing, does the same. Another bird device to prevent stalling is the shouldered wing-tip feathers, which spill through the wing tips and prevent eddies creeping across the wing (Figure 6-1).

Stability in flight is largely a matter of center of gravity. In birds and in the space shuttle, the body is slung below the wings to give a low center of gravity. This also prevents rolling in flight. Birds differ from aircraft in having most of this weight behind the lifting point of the wings (Figure 6-2). This lets them turn easily. They can maneuver quickly to capture food. They also have a lower stalling speed, since they can spread and lower the tail in landing. A long tail, as in a kite, gives stability by lowering the center of gravity and providing a longer pitching axis with less sudden reaction.

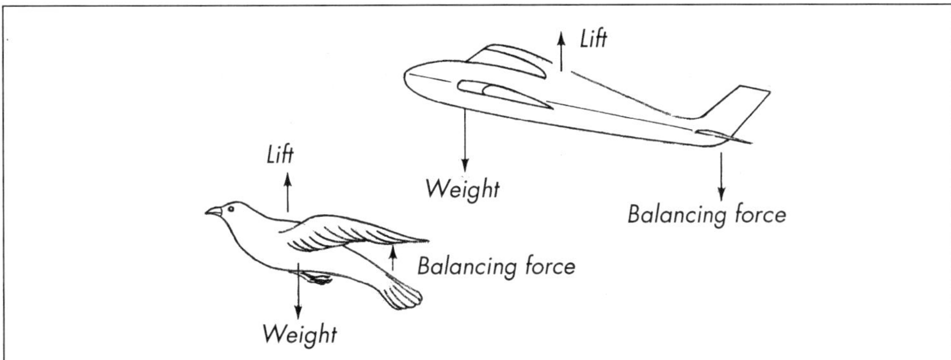

Figure 6-2. Balancing in flight requires a low center of gravity in both aircraft and birds.

Photo 2. The space shuttle Atlantis touches down at Edwards Air Force Base after reentry through the earth's atmosphere. What factors help with the shuttle's stability and control?

Looking at Air Movement and Center of Gravity

You can see how shape affects air movement and how keeping the weight low (a low center of gravity) favors stability.

What you need: candle, 5-cm-square card, piece of thick paper about 15 × 20 cm, apple, half-apple, bottle, two forks, needle, hat pin or ordinary pin, bottle with cork, string, pencil, slice of apple or potato

1. Light the candle and hold a card about 5 cm square between it and you. Blow hard against the card. What do you see the flame do (Figure 6-3)?

Figure 6-3. What happens to the flame?

2. Now fold the piece of thick paper into a cigar or torpedo shape. Blow at the flame, holding the torpedo shape in place of the card. What is the result? Explain why (Figure 6-4).

Figure 6-4. What happens to the flame now?

3. Now try some other shapes—an apple, a half-apple, a bottle. Experiment with these and the folded paper until you find a shape that blows the flame away from you in the most even manner. Draw the streamlines, the eddy currents.

4. Can you balance a needle on the top of a pin? Try it by pushing the needle through the apple and pushing two forks into the apple as in Figure 6-5. What does this do to the center of gravity? Is most of the weight below or above the needle point? Try turning the forks upward or outward. Can you get the arrangement to balance?

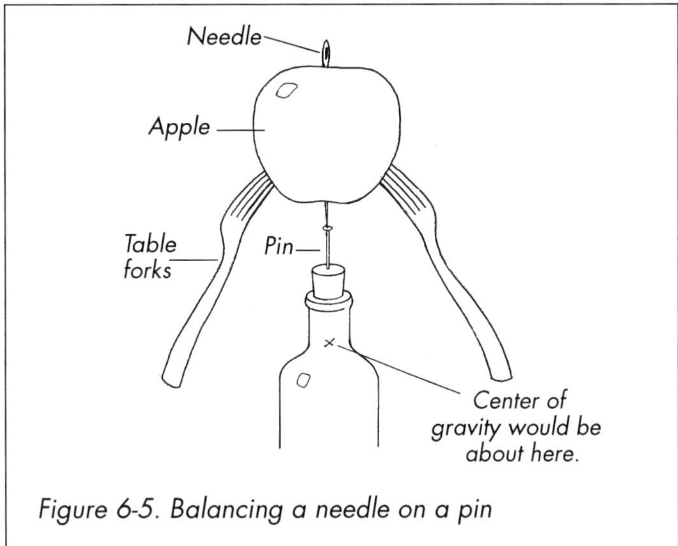

Figure 6-5. Balancing a needle on a pin

5. Try balancing a pencil on your desk edge as in Figure 6-6. Where is the center of gravity? Where would it be in the space shuttle—in the nose, or in the front of the wings?

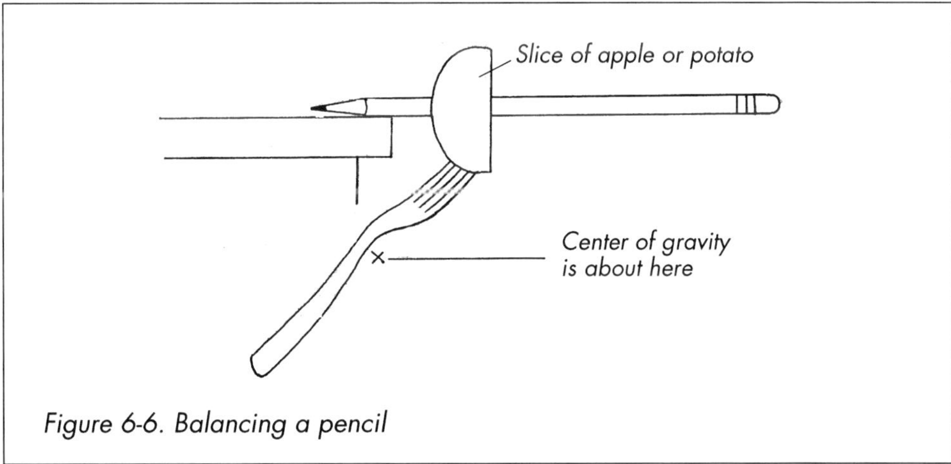

Figure 6-6. Balancing a pencil

7. Deceleration Problems

Scientists have done a great deal of research to ensure the successful return of a spacecraft through the earth's atmosphere. Heat from friction is a major problem, but new materials help take care of this. Communication is also an issue. During reentry into the earth's atmosphere, the spacecraft is surrounded by a layer of ionized—or electrically charged—air that blacks out radio talk.

The astronaut's safety is another major problem. The spacecraft is entering the denser atmosphere at about 30,000 kilometers per hour. Retro-rockets fire to decelerate the spacecraft; the astronaut experiences forces that increase his weight up to eight times. Specially designed couches help the astronaut withstand the tremendous pressures of deceleration.

Observing Deceleration

You may experiment with the effects of deceleration.

What you need: shoe box, toy trolley or roller skate, doll, string, marbles, plastic cup, brick

1. To study the effects of deceleration, tie the shoe box to a toy trolley or roller skate. Put the doll in the back end of the box and push the skate across the floor to hit the brick. What happens (Figure 7-1)?

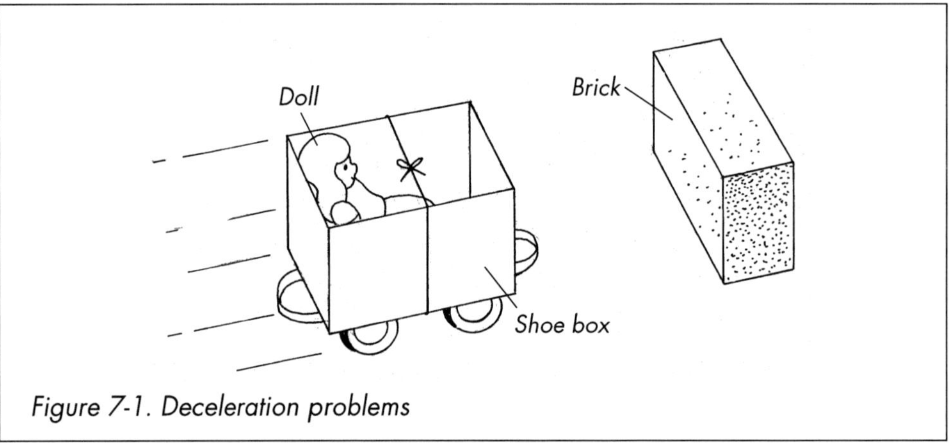

Figure 7-1. Deceleration problems

2. Now sit the doll with its back next to the front end of the box and push the skate as before. What difference in behavior do you note? How is this like the astronaut in a spacecraft during reentry into the earth's atmosphere?

3. Put marbles in a cup. Move the cup along a table, then stop suddenly. How do the marbles behave? Explain why. How does this help illustrate the problems of deceleration that astronauts face (Figure 7-2)?

Figure 7-2. Stop the movement suddenly.

8. Flight Paths

You can make curves called conic sections by cutting or making a section of a cone. An ellipse is an egg-shaped curve. A special type of ellipse is a circle. In a parabola, the two sides, if extended, never meet. The curve for a hyperbola is always two identical branches (Figure 8-1).

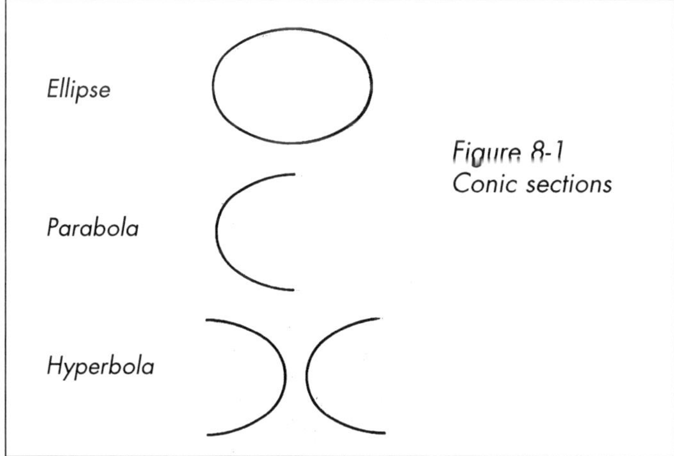

An easy way to make a parabola is to toss a coin or ball into the air. The path of any object moving freely in a gravity field is always a parabola. Air resistance may distort the path.

Reflectors like radar dishes that track spacecraft and rockets are often parabolic in shape. A car headlight is parabolic. If the lighted bulb is located at the focus of the parabolic reflector, the reflected rays form a parallel beam (Figure 8-2).

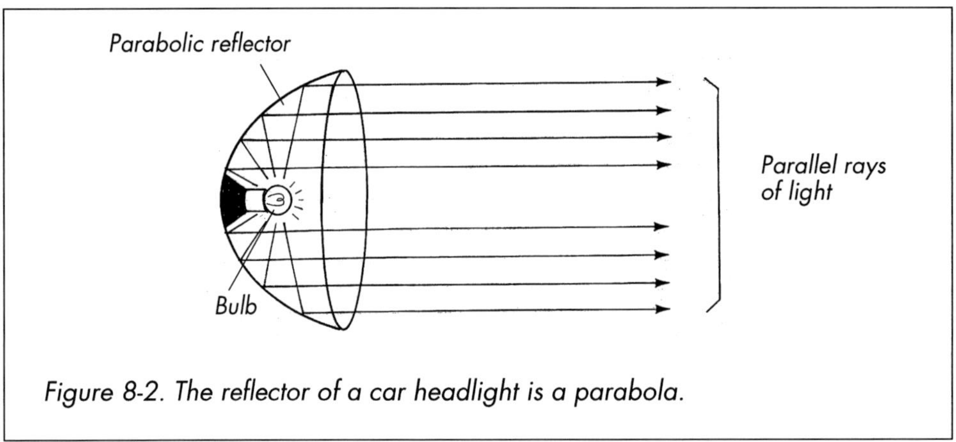

Figure 8-2. The reflector of a car headlight is a parabola.

Parabolas are of interest to astronomers as telescope mirrors and comet orbits. About half of all comets observed have a parabolic path.

Making Conic Sections

The hyperbola is an open curve. It is the path followed by a celestial body that passes another celestial body but is not captured into orbit around it. In contrast to the open curves of hyperbolas and parabolas, circles and ellipses are closed curves. The orbits of earth satellites are ellipses.

You can make the four conic section curves—**circle**, **ellipse**, **parabola**, and **hyperbola**.

What you need: paper or light cardboard cone, scissors

1. To make a paper cone, fold the sheet of paper or card as shown. Paste or tape the free edges. Trim as necessary so that your cone stands upright (Figure 8-3).

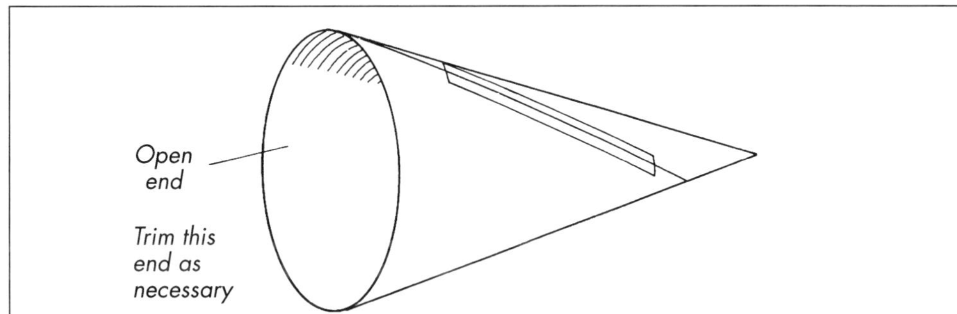

Figure 8-3. Making the cone. Roll a large sheet of paper to give you a kind of megaphone or cone. Seal the free end of the paper (or card) with tape. Then trim the open end so that your cone stands upright.

2. Now make a cut parallel to the base. What kind of a curve do you get? In launching a spacecraft, it is almost impossible to make the rocket give just the right amount of push so that the spacecraft makes a perfect circle (Figure 8-4).

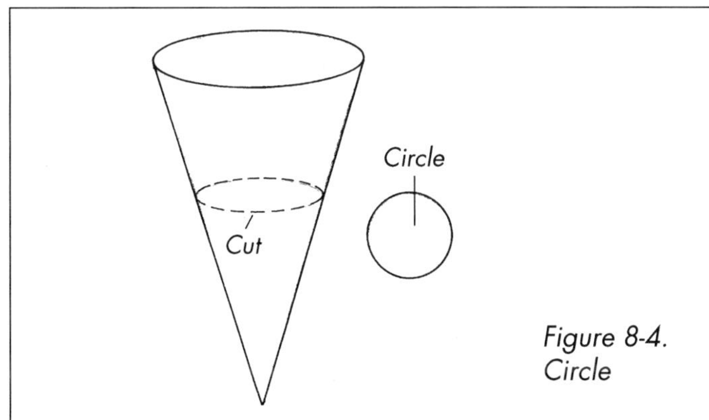

Figure 8-4. Circle

(continued)

Making Conic Sections *(continued)*

3. To be sure a spacecraft will orbit, engineers design rockets to give extra push. This sends the spacecraft out into an egg-shaped path called an ellipse. To make your ellipse, cut your cone as in Figure 8-5.

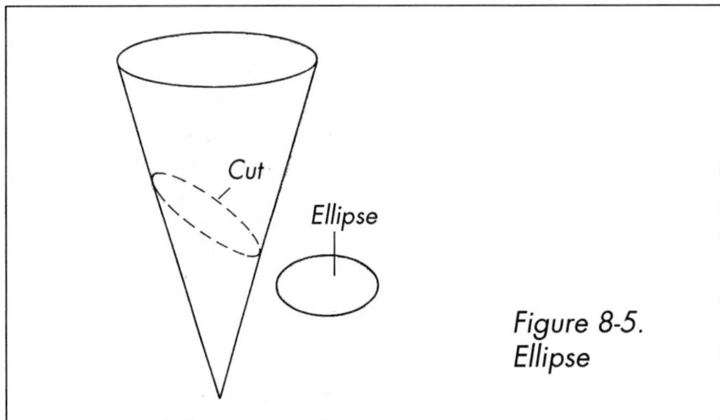

4. To make your parabola and hyperbola, make cuts as shown in Figures 8-6 and 8-7.

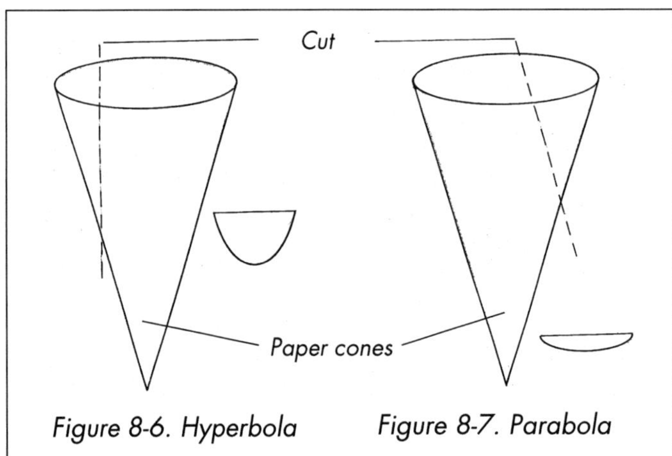

5. Label your curves and arrange as a display. Add some notes telling how they are important to astronomers.

(continued)

Making Conic Sections *(continued)*

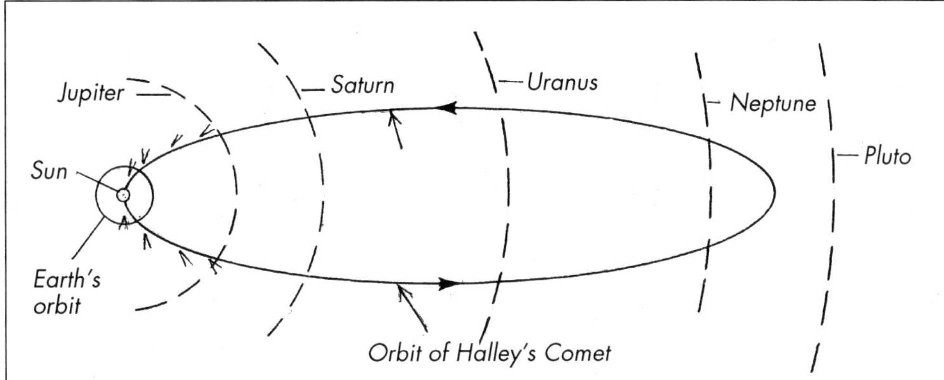

Figure 8-8. The orbit of Halley's Comet is an ellipse that reaches out nearly as far as Pluto, the most distant planet of the solar system. As the comet approaches the sun, its tail begins to grow.

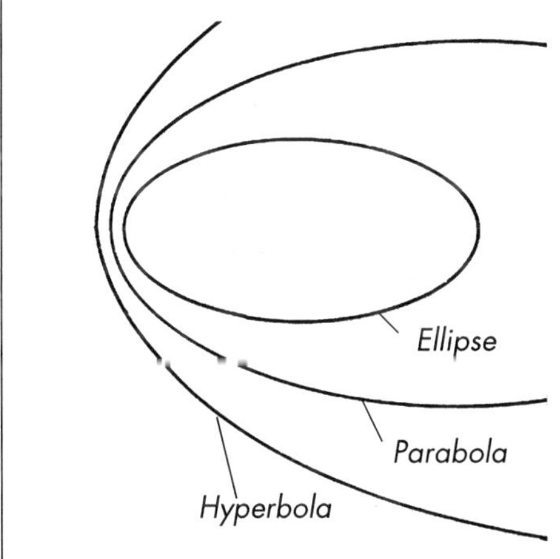

Figure 8-9. It is possible that all comet orbits were ellipses at one time. But the gravity pulls of planets have deviated many of them so that now they are parabolas or hyperbolas. Comets having these orbits will not return.

9. Into Orbit/Geosynchronous Orbit

Putting a satellite into orbit is rather like throwing a stone—it flies through the air, then falls back to ground, as in drawing A (Figure 9-1). When you throw it harder (drawing B), it flies farther through the air before friction with the air slows it down and gravity pulls it back to earth. Pretend you throw it so hard that it keeps on going forward just about as far as it falls (drawing C).

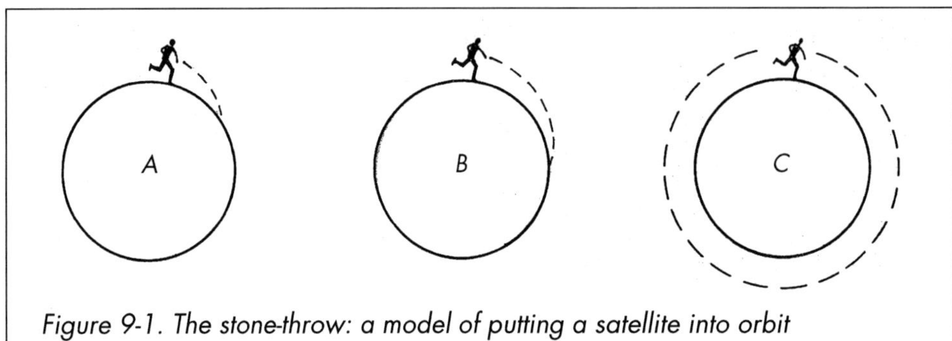

Figure 9-1. The stone-throw: a model of putting a satellite into orbit

The stone keeps curving downward but it does not reach earth. Rather it makes a great circle around earth. If there is enough atmosphere, friction slows it down. Gravity then takes over and pulls it back to earth. For this reason, real satellites must be launched to heights above significant effects from the atmosphere.

In space, the satellite follows an egg-shaped path called an ellipse. The point closest to earth is called the perigee of the orbit; the point farthest from earth is the apogee. In the activity on the following page, there is friction between the plastic cap and the support wire. This slows the "satellite," gravity takes over, and it plunges back to "earth."

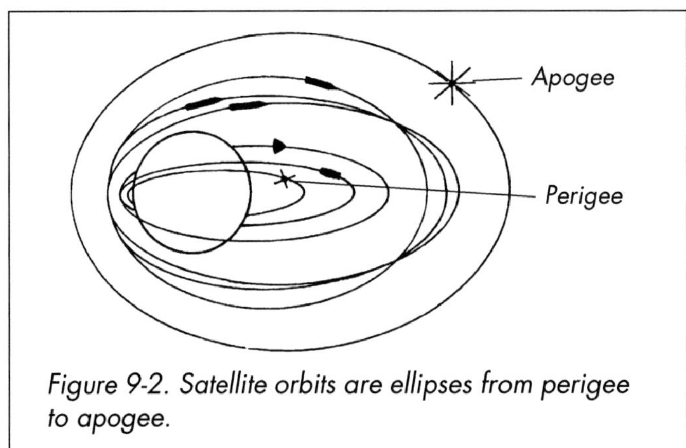

Figure 9-2. Satellite orbits are ellipses from perigee to apogee.

A real satellite, like the apple of Sir Isaac Newton, also falls to earth, burning up like a meteor as it flashes downward through the dense layers of the atmosphere.

Observing Satellite Orbits

You can make a "satellite launcher" and observe orbits. You will see how speed, gravity, and friction affect them.

What you need: large ball, strong 50-cm wire, 50-cm string, weight, 15-cm tube, 12 washers, plastic top of felt-tip marker, tape, bucket

1. Set up your satellite launcher as shown. What does the ball represent? What does the lead sinker represent (Figure 9-3)?

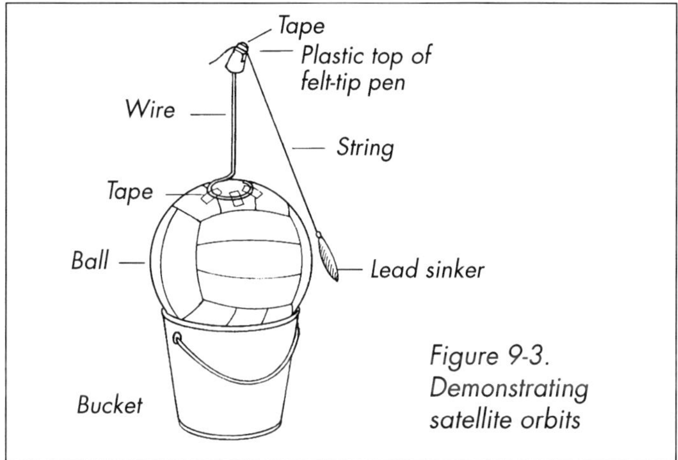

Figure 9-3. Demonstrating satellite orbits

2. Lift the "satellite" a little up and away from "earth" and release. What happens? What force acts on the satellite (Figure 9-4)?

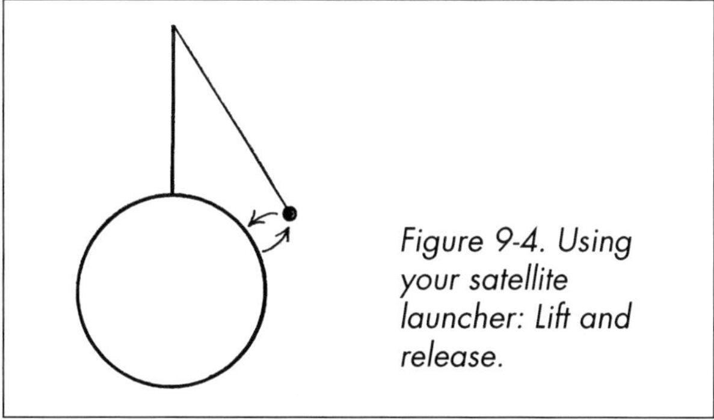

Figure 9-4. Using your satellite launcher: Lift and release.

3. Give the satellite a forward tap, pushing it away from the earth at an angle. Note how far the satellite travels (Figure 9-5). What if its speed had been a little greater? Try it (Figure 9-6). What helps the satellite to overcome gravity? What slows it down? What decides how far the satellite travels?

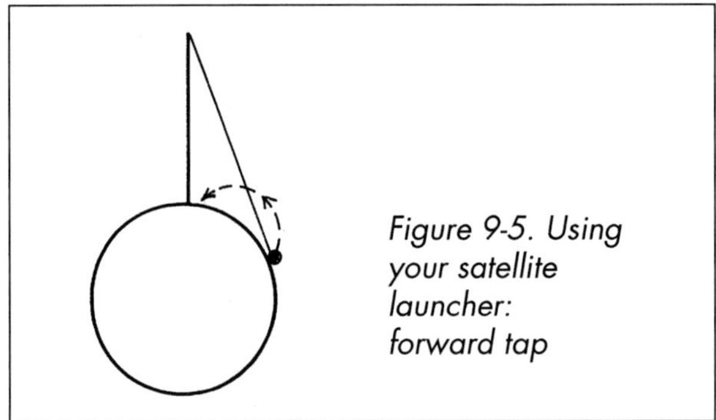

Figure 9-5. Using
your satellite
launcher:
forward tap

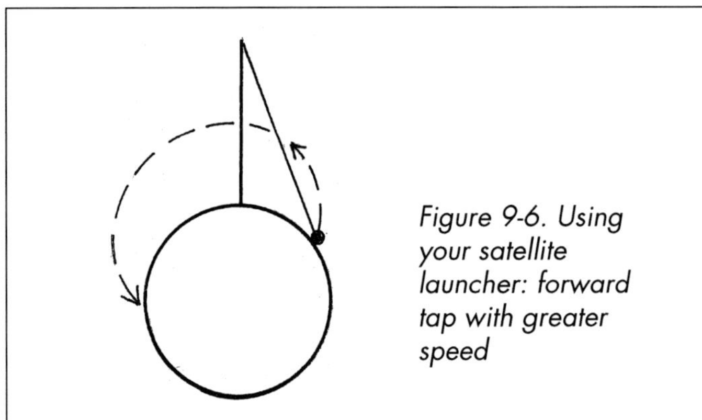

Figure 9-6. Using
your satellite
launcher: forward
tap with greater
speed

4. Give the satellite a forward push so that it goes into orbit around earth (Figure 9-7).
    What is the name for the satellite's path? Where is the apogee? The perigee? What
    happens as the satellite slows down? How do speed, gravity, and friction affect
    orbits? Write a paragraph telling how.

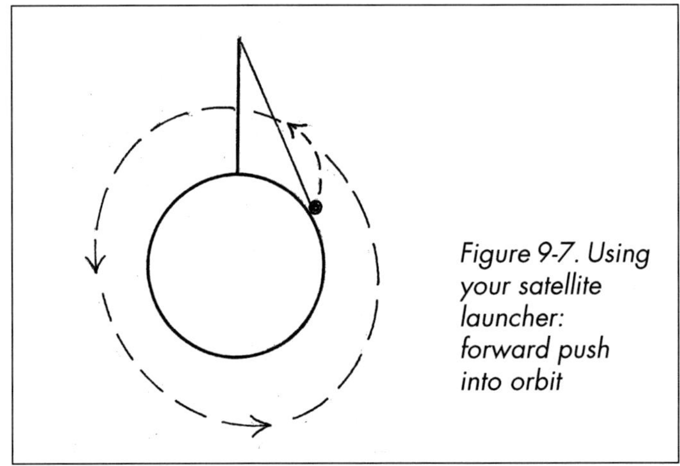

Figure 9-7. Using
your satellite
launcher:
forward push
into orbit

5. To experiment further with the forces acting on a satellite in earth orbit, use the setup shown in Figure 9-8. Hold the tube overhead in one hand and support the 10-washer weight with the other. Then set the small weight swinging in a horizontal circle. What happens as you increase its speed? Is the large weight lifted? What can you say about the centrifugal effect (acting to lift the weight) and centripetal force or gravity (holding the small object in its circular path)?

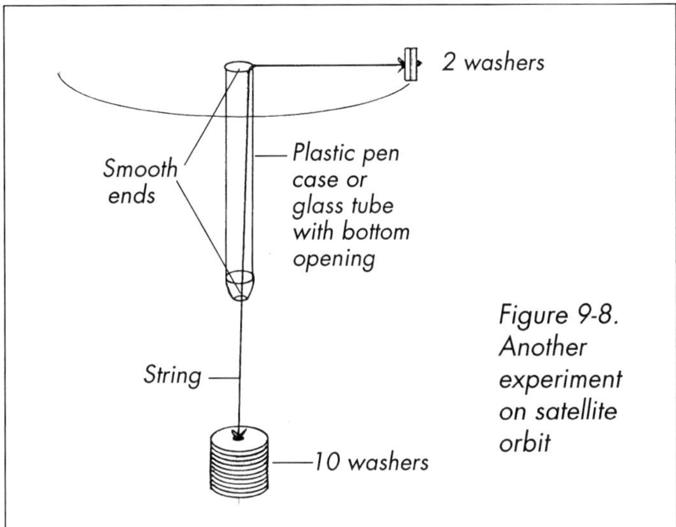

Figure 9-8. Another experiment on satellite orbit

6. How is the setup above like the curved path of a planet in orbit around the sun?

Geosynchronous Orbit

You can investigate the altitude at which a satellite must be placed in orbit so that it always remains above the same point on the earth. This is called geosynchronous orbit. To be useful for communication, a satellite must be placed in such an orbit so it will always be in the same position with respect to ground-based transmitting and receiving stations. Since the space shuttle orbits at only 500 km to 600 km above the earth, a communication satellite deployed by the space shuttle must have a secondary booster rocket to launch it to the required height.

The altitude for geosynchronous orbit is specific and depends on Newton's Law of Universal Gravitation. When the force of gravity acting on the satellite exactly equals the centripetal force necessary to hold the satellite in orbit at exactly the rotational speed of the earth, the satellite is geosynchronous.

What you need: a scientific calculator

1. The following data are required to make the calculation:

   Mass of the earth: $M_e = 5.98 \times 10^{24}$ kg
   Radius of the earth: $r_e = 6.38 \times 10^3$ km
   Gravitational constant: $G = 6.67 \times 10^{-20}$ km^3 s^{-2} kg^{-1}

2. These formulas will be needed to make the calculation:

   Law of Universal Gravitation: $F = G\, m\, M_e / r^2$ (where m is the mass of the satellite and r is the distance to the center of the earth)

   Centripetal force on an object in motion around a central point: $F = m\, v^2 / r$ (where v is the speed the satellite is travelling in its orbit around the center of the earth)

   For geosynchronous orbit, these forces are equal, so $G\, m\, M_e / r^2 = m\, v^2 / r$. In number 4 below, you will solve for r, the distance to the center of the earth. If you subtract the radius of the earth (r_e), you will have the altitude of geosynchronous orbit!

3. On the previous page, you showed how an object swinging on a string in a horizontal circle could lift more weight as it was swung faster. For this calculation, you need to know how fast a geosynchronous satellite travels in its orbit about the center of the earth. How many seconds are there in one day? _______________________________________. The satellite's speed depends on how fast the earth is turning and the distance of the satellite above the center of the earth. Apply the formula for the circumference of a circle, and use the number of seconds in a day to find a formula for the speed: $v = 2\pi r / T$ (where T is the number of seconds in a day).

4. Now, you need to do some algebra to solve for r. Show that $r = \sqrt[3]{(G\, M_e\, T^2 / 4\pi^2)}$:

5. Calculate: $r = \sqrt[3]{[(G = 6.67 \times 10^{-20})(5.98 \times 10^{24})(T^2) / (4\pi^2)]} = $ ___________________________

6. Subtract r_e from r to find the altitude: $h = $ _____________ (3.59×10^4 km or 2.23×10^4 mi)

32 *Space Science: 44 Activities, Experiments, and Projects*

10. Inertia Wheels

Inertia is the tendency of a body at rest to stay at rest and the tendency of a body that is moving to keep moving in the same straight line unless some other force acts on it.

In the experiments that follow, the inertia of the coin keeps it at rest when the card is flicked away. Gravity then causes the coin to fall into the glass. Results are similar for the paper hoop.

Uncontrolled spacecraft tumble erratically in orbit. Inertia wheels (gyroscopes) are among many types of devices used by space scientists to stabilize or align a spacecraft so that a particular experiment sensor can point in a desired direction. Scientists may turn the spacecraft to point at a new target with earth-based ground or programmed onboard computers.

Inertia wheels depend on Newton's third law of motion: For every action there is an equal and opposite reaction. A person steps out of a canoe (action) and so imparts an opposite motion (reaction) to the canoe. In the same way, if an electric motor is used to increase the turning speed of an inertia wheel in direction W, an opposite torque or turning motion is given to the motor mount (Figure 10-1). This causes the spacecraft structure and attached sensor to turn in direction M. During this swing, the inertia wheel is made to decelerate at a rate which slows the spacecraft's turn and stops it with the sensor exactly on target.

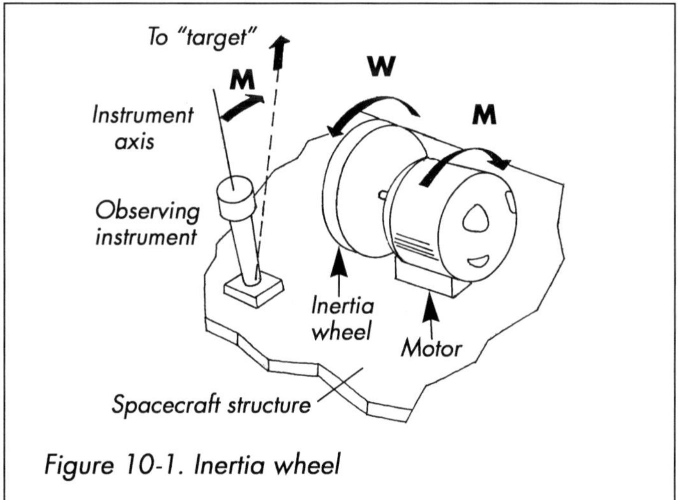

Figure 10-1. Inertia wheel

The same process then works to hold the sensor on target despite various disturbance forces on the spacecraft. Some originate within the spacecraft (for example, moving machinery) while others come from outside (micrometeoroids, solar wind pressure).

Accelerating and decelerating the wheel will allow many alignments of the spacecraft. However, the wheel may reach its maximum allowed rotational speed. From then on, it can only be used to turn the spacecraft in one direction—the one obtained by decelerating the wheel. To regain usefulness for both directions, its rotational energy must be lessened. Gas jets are used to produce an opposite, steadying torque on the spacecraft while the speed is slowed.

Investigating Inertia

You may investigate inertia, the natural tendency of a body to remain stationary or to keep moving once in motion.

What you need: coin, card, glass, paper strip, staples, 10-cm cardboard disk cut from thick cardboard, plastic cap of felt-tip pen, 10-cm nail, string, empty thread spool, contact adhesive, toy gyroscope

1. Place the coin on the card over the glass as shown in Figure 10-2. Now give the coin a sharp flick. What happens—to the card, to the coin? Explain why. How does inertia come into it?

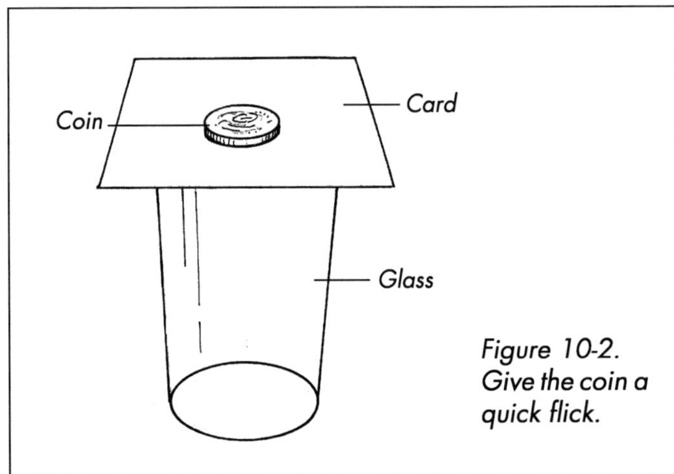

Figure 10-2.
Give the coin a
quick flick.

2. Make a paper hoop and place the coin on this as in Figure 10-3. Now pull the hoop sharply away. What happens to the coin? Explain how inertia is involved.

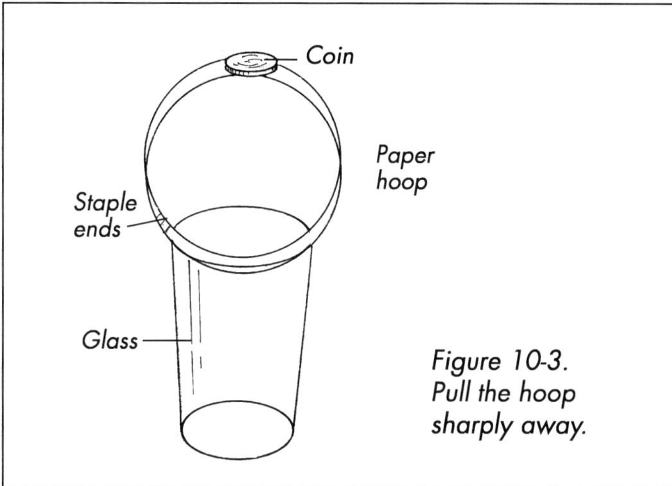

Figure 10-3.
Pull the hoop
sharply away.

3. Put the nail through the spool. Then fix the tip of the nail to the inside of the plastic pen top with adhesive. Complete the arrangement shown in Figure 10-4. Make sure the disk fits snugly around the pen top. Wind the string firmly around the nail 3–4 times before tying it tightly; then wind the rest of the string around the nail.

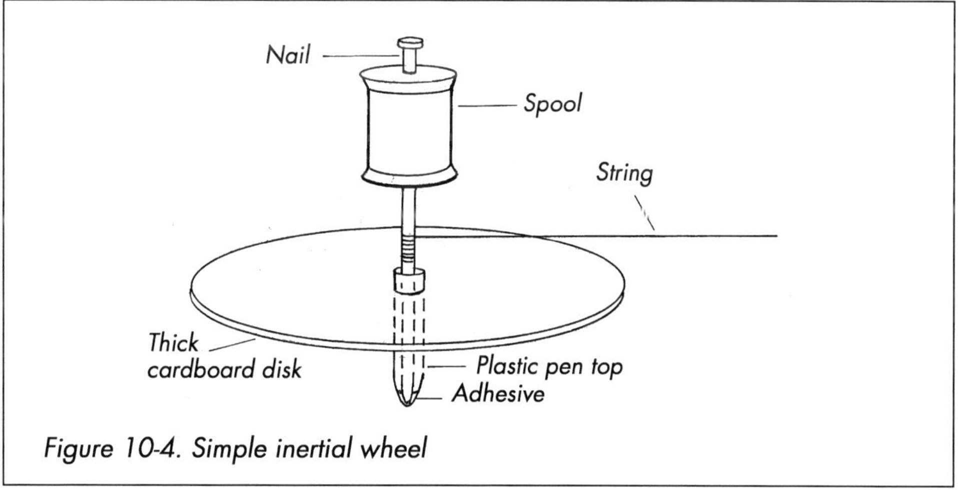

Figure 10-4. Simple inertial wheel

4. Hold the spool and pull on the string at the proper intervals to rotate the system first in one direction and then in the other. What keeps the disk spinning after you stop pulling on the string? What winds up the string in the reverse direction?

5. Experiment with the toy gyroscope (Figure 10-5). Note that it appears to defy the law of gravity. When you set the gyroscope spinning, observe the direction of spin of the wheel. Now turn the gyroscope upside down. What direction is the wheel revolving in now? How much work do you have to do? What finally causes the spinning gyroscope to fall over?

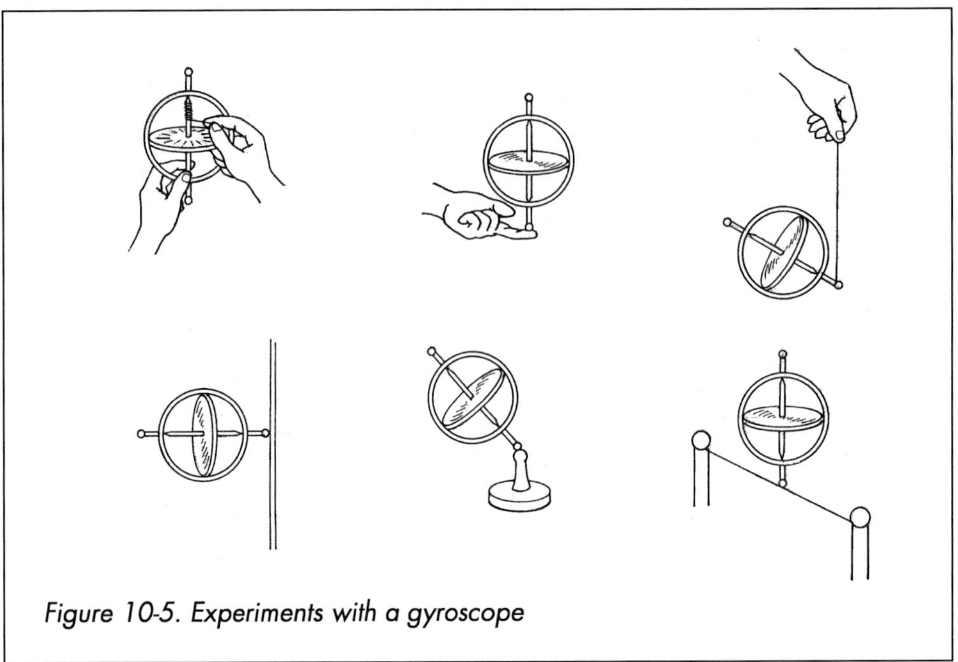

Figure 10-5. Experiments with a gyroscope

11. Airflow and Guidance Vanes

When you blow against the can in the experiment that follows, the airstream divides around the can, each half producing low pressure between itself and the can. This follows from Bernoulli's principle, which explains how a rapid stream of gas or liquid produces low pressure in the space nearby. The pressure of a moving gas decreases as its velocity increases. Each half-stream is pressed against the can by the greater air pressure on its outer side.

With two cans and three cans, the airstream divides as before and is held to the cans as explained above. On the far side of the can, the two streams come together and blow out the candle.

With the funnel, your airstream hugs the inner side. Again, because of low pressure in the stream, atmospheric pressure pushes it against the side. The airstream leaves the funnel as a kind of cone with low air pressure at the center. Air flowing into this low-pressure region carries the flame toward you. Airflow at the edge of the funnel blows the flame away from you.

"Vane" is a general term for a thin, flat, or curved metal section over which air or gas can flow freely. Vanes may be fixed in place. Or they may pivot to align themselves with fluid direction. Vanes have uses as stator blades in compressors or turbines and are also used in wind tunnels.

Just as fish have fins for steering, so also do rockets and spacecraft such as the space shuttle. Fins or guidance vanes act as flight controls—rather like the rudder of an aircraft. The smooth flow of fluid across fin or vane helps to confer stability in motion or flight.

Steering by jet means using fixed or movable gas jets on a rocket or spacecraft to steer it along a desired path during propelled and coasting flight.

Experimenting with Airflow

You can experiment with airflow and guidance vanes.

What you need: three same-size small cans, candle, funnel, light cardboard, thread, paper airplane, cardboard mailing tube, scissors, drinking straw

1. Place a can on the table with a burning candle about 5 cm behind it. With your mouth about 5 cm in front of the can, blow hard against it. What happens to the candle (Figure 11-1)? How does the shape of the can help the airflow?

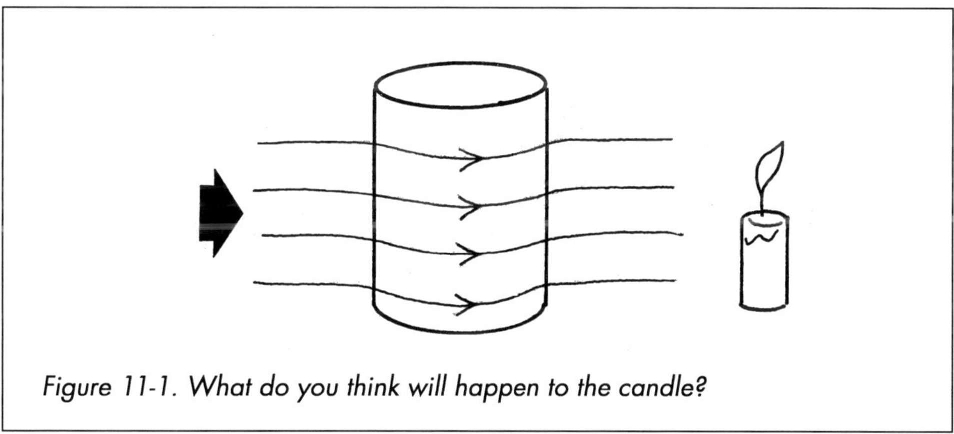

Figure 11-1. What do you think will happen to the candle?

2. Repeat with two cans, then three cans. What do you find (Figure 11-2)?

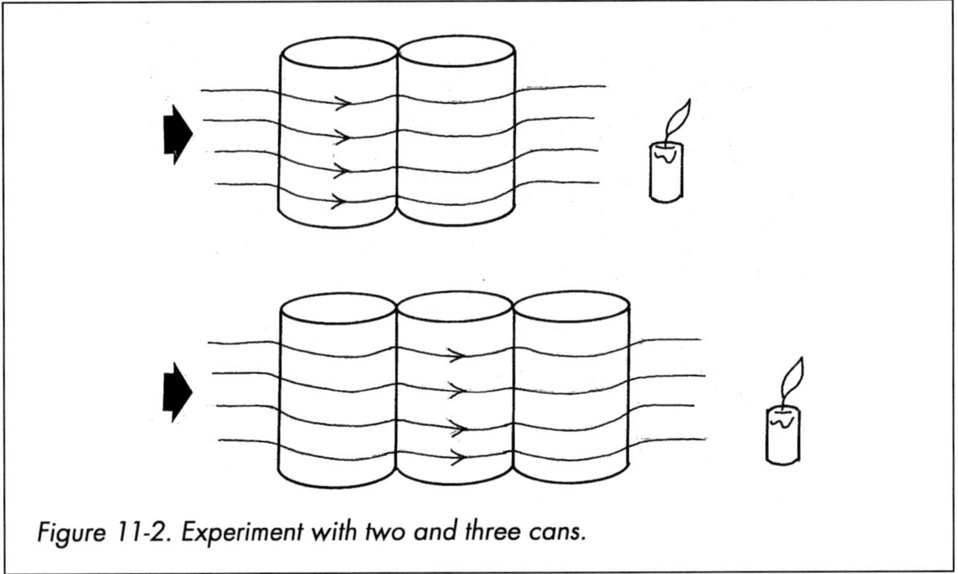

Figure 11-2. Experiment with two and three cans.

3. Blow into the small end of the plastic funnel, holding the candle in the approximate position indicated in the diagram. What do you notice about the flame? Repeat, holding the flame opposite the rim of the funnel. How does the flame behave this time? Explain this in terms of airstreams (Figure 11-3).

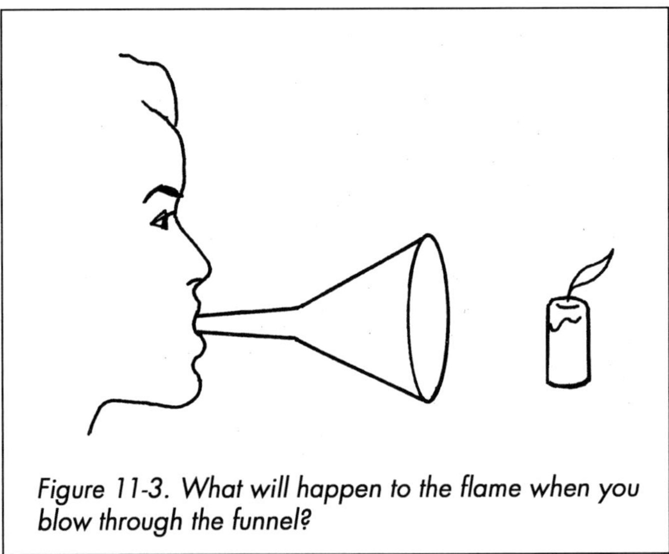

Figure 11-3. What will happen to the flame when you blow through the funnel?

4. Cut out a model rocket from light cardboard and tie it to a thread as in Figure 11-4. Pull this upward through the air, observing its motion in flight. Now experiment with bending the control vanes. Explain the changes in motion.

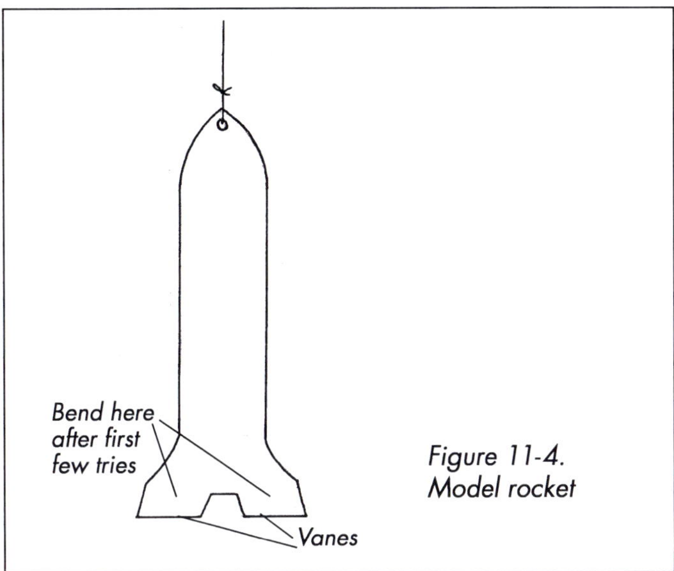

Figure 11-4.
Model rocket

5. Try this also with a paper airplane. Turn the back ends down slightly, launch, and note what happens in flight. Then turn one end up a little and one end down and launch. Does your airplane perform a roll? How are "vanes" helping? Now turn both ends up slightly. How does your airplane fly this time? Would a jet in flight perform the same way (Figure 11-5)?

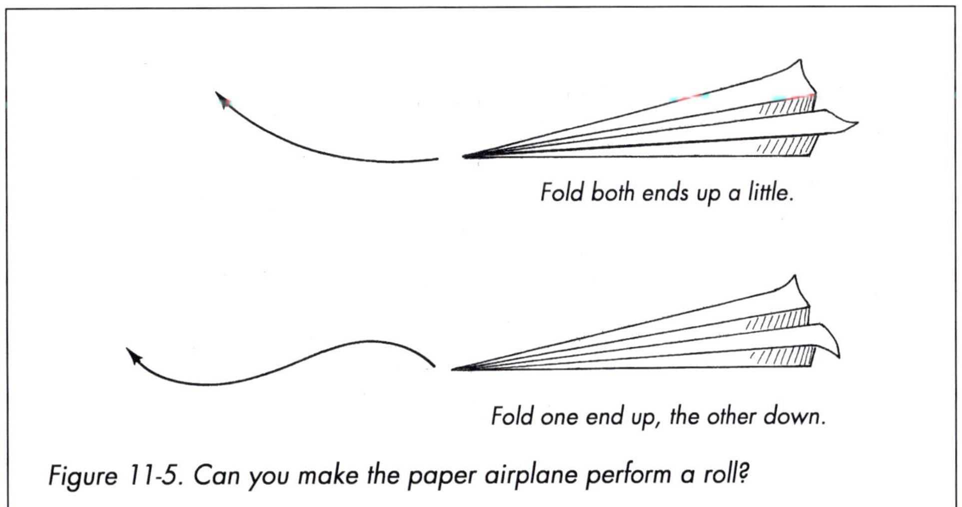

Figure 11-5. Can you make the paper airplane perform a roll?

6. Steering by jet: To show this, make cuts in the end of the cardboard mailing tube.
   In the slits, insert a vertical fin or vane cut from light cardboard. Hang the tube by
   a thread as in Figure 11-6, then blow through the tube with the drinking straw.
   Blow first from one side, then from the other. Describe how the tube changes direction as the airstream strikes the guidance vane. Try bending the vane one way or
   other, then blowing into the tube. How is direction affected?

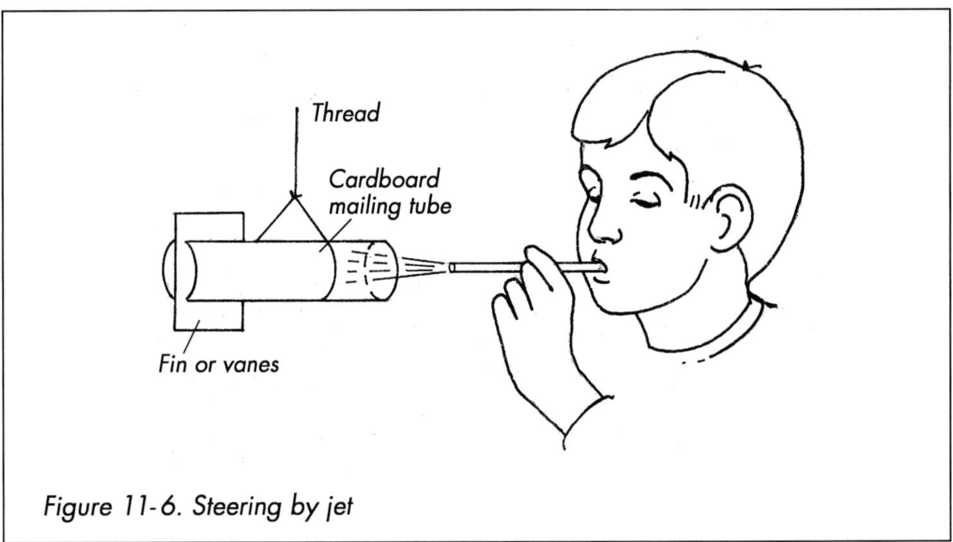

Figure 11-6. Steering by jet

CHAPTER TWO

SPACE VEHICLES

12. Magnetic Control

> *But I am constant as the northern star,*
> *Of whose true-fix'd and resting quality*
> *There is no fellow in the firmament.*
>
> —William Shakespeare (*Julius Caesar*)

Scientists discovered that there were mysterious small changes in the attitude (position) of one of the weather satellites in orbit around the earth. They traced the changes to the influence of the earth's magnetism on the magnetic field created by the satellite's electrical equipment. With the idea of using these magnetic forces to their advantage, scientists designed a magnetic attitude control coil for the next weather satellite. Its purpose was to change the pointing direction of the satellite so that they could study areas of particular interest. In addition, the coil ensured that the angle between the sun, the earth, and the satellite was correct.

Aluminum wire of 250 turns around the base of the satellite made up the magnetic control coil. When electric current flows through the coil, it becomes a magnet with its own magnetic field. The flow of electric current is controlled by the ground station. Reversing the flow through the coil reverses the direction of the field. The effect is to make the coil behave like a compass needle, lining up with the earth's magnetic field. The law of magnetism says like poles repel, unlike poles attract. As the forces concerned are very small, the magnetic effect causes a very slow change in the tilt of the satellite—less than one degree per orbit. This control system is very fine. It has no moving parts and little power is needed, so a long period of usefulness is assured (Figure 12-1).

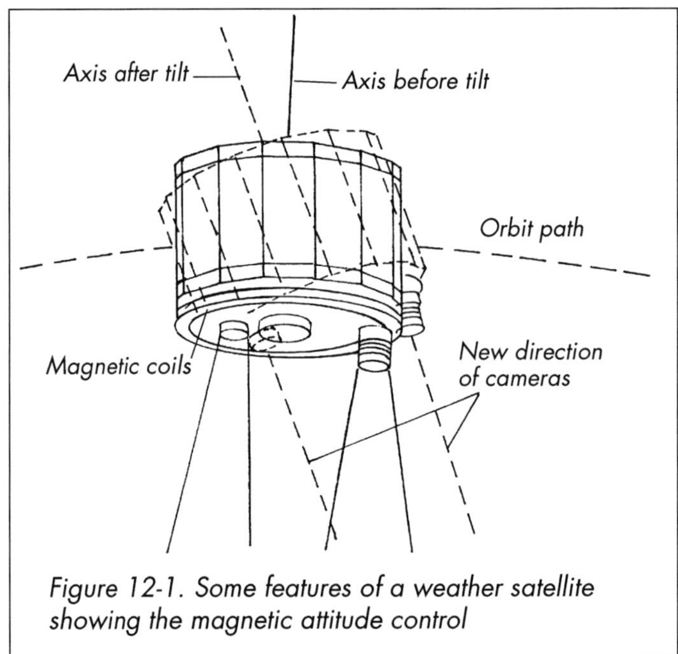

Figure 12-1. Some features of a weather satellite showing the magnetic attitude control

Photo 3. Cyclonic storm photographed by weather satellite

Exploring Magnetic Control

You can demonstrate magnetic control in this experiment.

What you need: ball of wool, magnetized knitting needle, small plastic bucket or carton, compass, insulated wire, nail, flashlight battery, string, bar magnet, tape, plasticene

1. The magnetic earth: Pass the magnetized knitting needle* through the ball of wool. This represents the earth and its invisible magnetic field. Set the ball of wool on top of the small bucket or carton. Move a compass around the ball. What controls the pointing direction or attitude of the needle? Explain how the compass shows direction. Can you state the law of magnetism (Figure 12-2)?

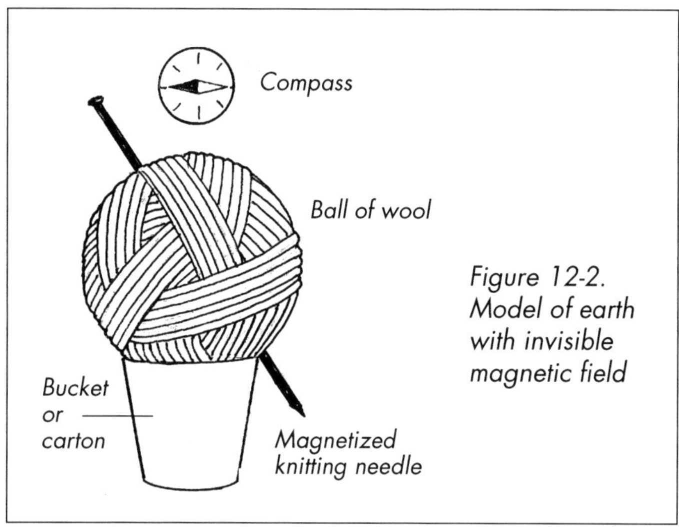

Figure 12-2.
Model of earth
with invisible
magnetic field

2. Magnetic attitude controls: Wind 12 turns of insulated wire around a nail. Tie the nail lengthwise to a flashlight battery with string. Bring the assembly up to a bar magnet (representing the earth's magnetic field) and move it around. The coil compares with that of the *Tiros* satellite that orbited the earth. In which direction does the nail point? Is it greatly affected by the field of the bar magnet (Figure 12-3)?

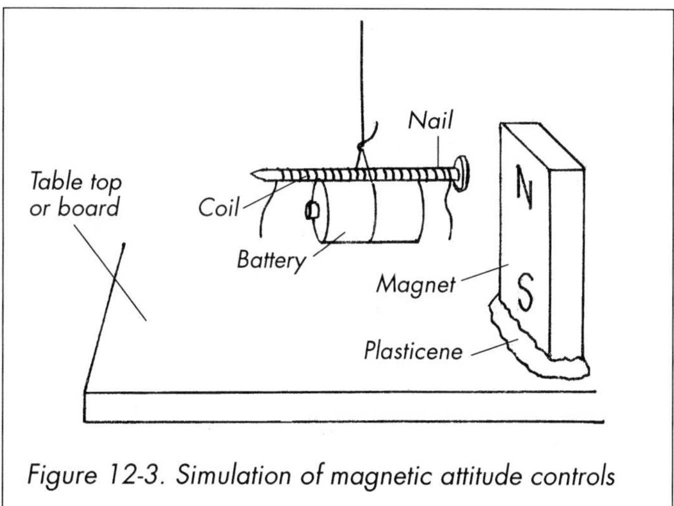

Figure 12-3. Simulation of magnetic attitude controls

---

* Magnetize the needle by stroking 20 times in one direction only with a bar magnet.

3. Remove about 2 cm of the insulation from each end of the coil wires and tape the ends to the battery terminals. What does the electric current do as it surges through the coil? How is the magnetic field of the coil affected by the field of the bar magnet? What can you say about the attitude the coil takes (how it points) in the field of the bar magnet? Can you explain why? How is this like the satellite in space?

4. Reverse the coil connections to the battery so that you reverse the flow of current through the coil, and repeat the experiment. Is the attitude of the device different? How? How is magnetic force used to control the attitude or pointing direction of a satellite in space? Write three or four sentences.

5. You receive a letter from a friend in another town who is also very interested in science. She writes: "I was told that even a plastic bag has magnetic properties, but I don't believe it. I could not pick up a plastic bag with a magnet when I tried it." How would you explain this puzzle to her?

13. Soft Landings

A spacecraft achieves a soft landing when it touches down at slow speed on a celestial body such as the moon or a planet. Usually there is no damage to the spacecraft. In the *Surveyor* series of space shots, a capsule packed with instruments soft-landed on the moon. A large rocket located centrally within *Surveyor* fired during descent to the moon; this acted as a "space brake" and allowed the spacecraft to touch down gently at about 8 kilometers/hour on the moon's surface. Landing legs on *Surveyor* permitted the spacecraft to stand upright and to absorb any shock on landing.

Instruments on *Surveyor* studied the moon's magnetism, temperatures, radiation, and atmosphere. Television cameras recorded details of the lunar landscape. A drill on *Surveyor* took samples of the lunar crust and passed them back into the spacecraft, where instruments analyzed them. The information about elements present on the moon was radioed back to earth.

Space probes such as the *Viking* Lander also investigated the possibility of life on Mars. On command from earth, a scoop moved out, took a sample of Martian soil, and passed it back into an automated laboratory within the spacecraft. Here it was tested for "little beasties"—bacteria, fungi spores. No form of life was found on Mars, however.

Making Soft Landings

You can imitate a soft landing or touchdown on the moon or Mars.

What you need: paper, scissors, handkerchief, thread, weight (washers), balloons, paper clips

1. Autogyros: Cut a 10×20-cm strip of paper (Figure 13-1). Fold this in half lengthwise and make a 10 cm cut up the middle. Fold the two flaps or wings in opposite directions, then make 3–4 folds in the keel. Stand on a table or chair; release your autogyro from as high as you can raise your hand. Describe how it comes down. Does it make a soft landing? Could spacecraft be designed with rotating wings so that they could touch down to a soft landing?

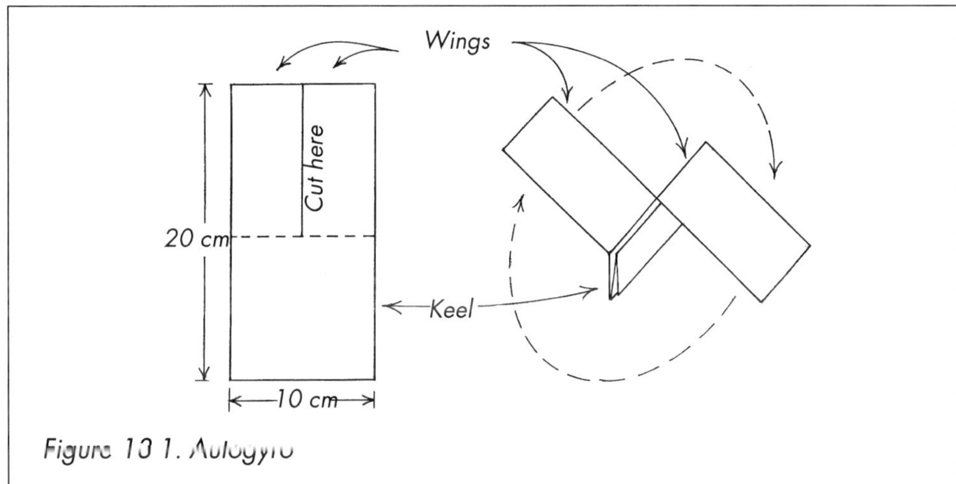

Figure 13-1. Autogyro

2. Parachute: Make a parachute from a large handkerchief, thread, and washers (Figure 13-2). When the parachute is scrunched into a bundle and thrown high, it unfolds and floats down slowly to a soft landing. How does the size of the handkerchief help to slow its downward fall? Find out how parachutes are used with spacecraft to help them touch down to a soft landing.

(continued)

Making Soft Landings *(continued)*

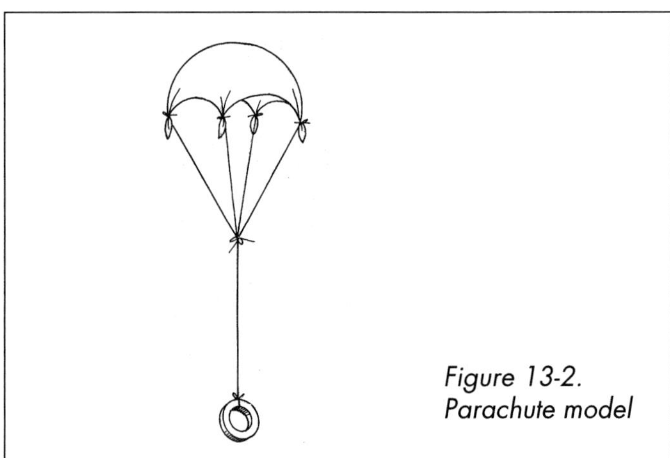

Figure 13-2.
Parachute model

3. Using a retro-rocket to brake for a soft landing: Blow up a toy balloon of the round type. Set it free without tying it off. Describe how it darts about. Which law of motion applies?

You can tame the balloon rocket and at the same time make an approximate measure of the thrust. Tie a 15-cm piece of thread to the neck of the balloon, but do not constrict the neck in any way. Hang paper clips as weights from a loop at the other end of the thread. If the weight is less than thrust, the balloon rises more or less evenly when you release it. When weight and thrust are about the same, the balloon hovers in midair as long as the air supply lasts. Weigh your paper clips. How many grams of thrust does the rubber balloon develop? To show retro-rocket action, add one or two more paper clips. Gravity will exceed thrust; you will see your retro-rocket make a soft landing on the table or chair. You can add to this mock-up with art to show the surface of the moon or Mars (Figure 13-3).

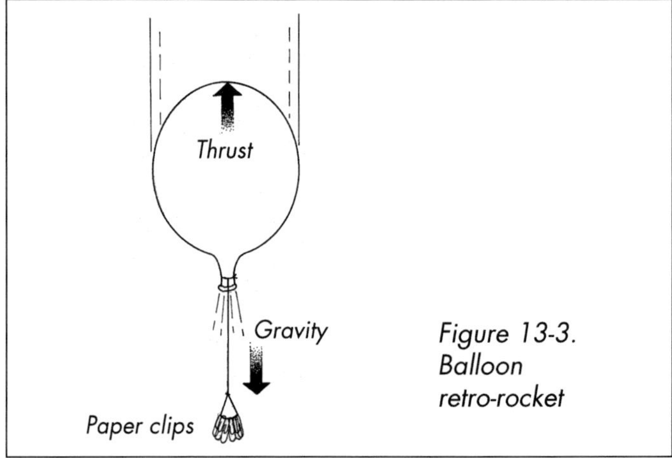

Figure 13-3.
Balloon
retro-rocket

14. Shapes for a Space Age

Topology is one of the newest and most exciting branches of geometry. Its importance is growing in vital fields such as electronics and aerodynamics (the science of flight). Topology deals with the properties of objects in space—points, lines, and shapes—and how they change. But topology only deals with those changes that do not include tearing, cutting, or folding of the figure.

Because topology deals with shapes and how they change, it is sometimes called "rubber sheet geometry." With topology, geometric figures may change in size and shape yet still keep certain properties. For example, if you draw a circle on a balloon, then blow up the balloon, the circle gets larger. Its shape changes as the rubber stretches. When you let the air out of the balloon you can stretch and twist the rubber circle, giving it different shapes and sizes. But no matter how you stretch or twist the rubber, you still have a simple closed curve. Topology tells us the figure is unchanged.

Topology is used in the design of the complex electronic equipment of spacecraft. It allows shapes and surfaces once thought impossible. The Möbius strip that you will make in this activity, for instance, has only one side and one edge. This surface from topology is used in spacecraft where no two parts must cross at any point.

Mysteries of the Möbius

You can make a Möbius strip, a favorite plaything of topologists, and explore its special properties.

What you need: paper, scissors, ruler, pencil, crayon, glue or tape

1. Cut a strip of paper, about 40 cm × 3 cm; use the template provided in Figure 14-1. About 1 cm from each end of the strip and on the same side of the paper, make a large dot with the crayon. Then give one end of the strip a half twist and paste the two ends together so that the two dots overlap at X (Figure 14-2). Your Möbius strip is now complete. Starting at X, draw a line with your pencil along the middle of the strip. Does your line pass below the starting point? If you continue the line, where do you come back to? Then how many sides does your strip have?

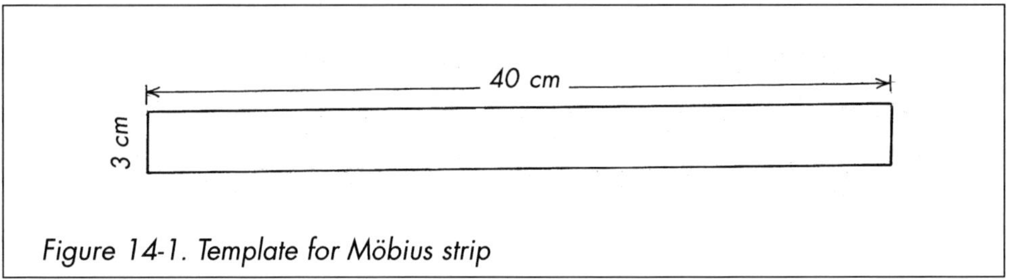

Figure 14-1. Template for Möbius strip

2. Draw another line near the edge of the strip. Do you come back to your starting point? What can you say about the edge of the strip? Is it continuous? How many edges are there?

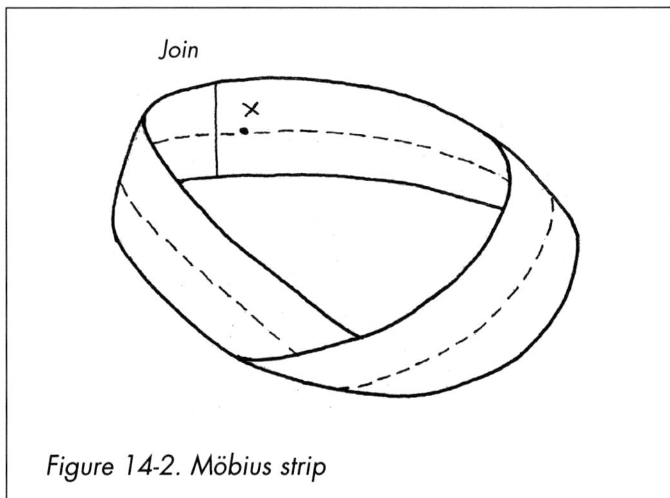

Figure 14-2. Möbius strip

(continued)

Mysteries of the Möbius *(continued)*

3. Cut the strip along the midline, starting at X. Would you expect to get two strips? But do you? Cut the strip along the middle again. Surely you will get two strips this time. But do you? Describe the special properties of your Möbius strip. Do some research: How is it used in spacecraft?

4. Try to color one side of the Möbius strip completely and not the other. Can you explain why is this not possible? Cut another Möbius strip along a line dividing it into one third and two thirds. What happens? Cut out another paper strip, but this time give it more twists before you paste it together. Cut as before. What is the result?

5. Another shape in topology is the Klein bottle. It has only one surface, which is like a sphere. It is completely closed; there is no inside or outside and no edges. Complex and intricate equipment can be packed in this arrangement, yet all parts can be gotten to equally. Find out anything else you can about a Klein bottle. What happens when a Klein bottle is cut in half? What do you get?

15. Shaped Reflectors

Shaped reflectors have been used for many years in lanterns, flashlights, car headlights, and searchlights. Today they are used in astronomy and astronautics as collectors of low-energy waves and as emitters of parallel waves.

Radio telescopes detect, receive, and record radiation from celestial bodies such as distant galaxies, and from space itself. The dish-shaped collectors receive the faint radio disturbances and concentrate them at a focal point so that they are strong enough to study and analyze. On earth we receive many radio waves from space that are of higher intensity than the background radiation, yet when an astronomer points her telescope at the same area, she can see nothing there. Astronomers say there are dark stars, which, while they cannot be seen, are powerful emitters of radio waves.

The dishes can also be used to send out a beam of waves to a distant object. The waves reflect from the object as in radar. Reflectors also are used to focus the sun's rays, producing temperatures of thousands of degrees.

For recording bird songs and detecting aircraft, large, similar, dish-shaped collectors and reflectors trap weak incoming signals. Band shells and dome-shaped roofs in buildings also work this way. In humans and many animals, the outer part of the ear acts as a very useful collector and reflector of waves, passing them into the canal of the ear, which leads to the eardrum.

Collecting and Reflecting Waves

You can use shaped reflectors to collect and reflect waves.

What you need: ticking watch or small clock, sheet of strong paper, tape, two umbrellas, string, chairs, bowl-shaped dish or plastic lampshade

1. Roll the sheet of paper to make a cone-shaped megaphone. Secure the free edge with tape.

2. Speak softly to a friend 2–3 meters away. Does your friend hear you? Have your friend hold the megaphone to his ear and point it at you. Speak again. Does your friend hear you better now? How are waves being collected and reflected? Can you draw the paths of the waves (Figure 15-1)?

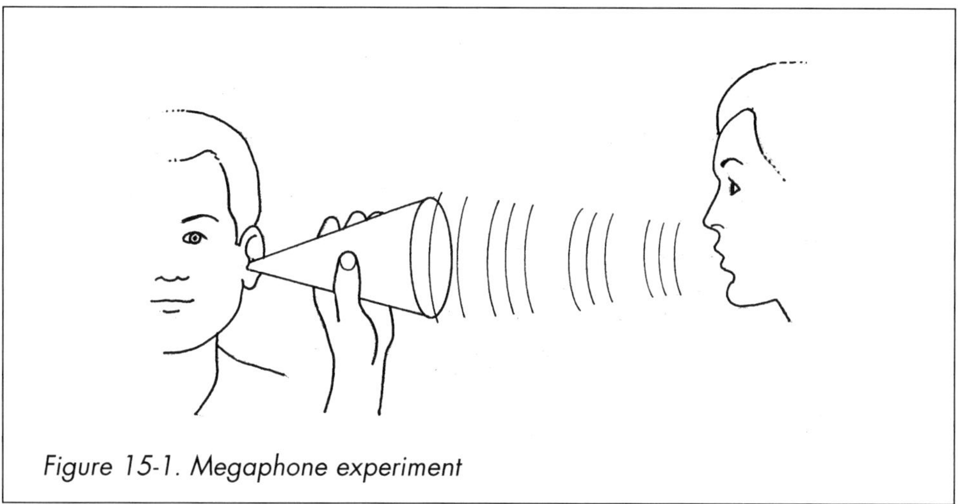

Figure 15-1. Megaphone experiment

3. Have your friend hold a watch near your ear, then move slowly away. How far away is he when you can no longer hear the ticking? Now have him hold the watch at the center of the bowl. How much farther can he move with you still hearing the tick (Figure 15-2)?

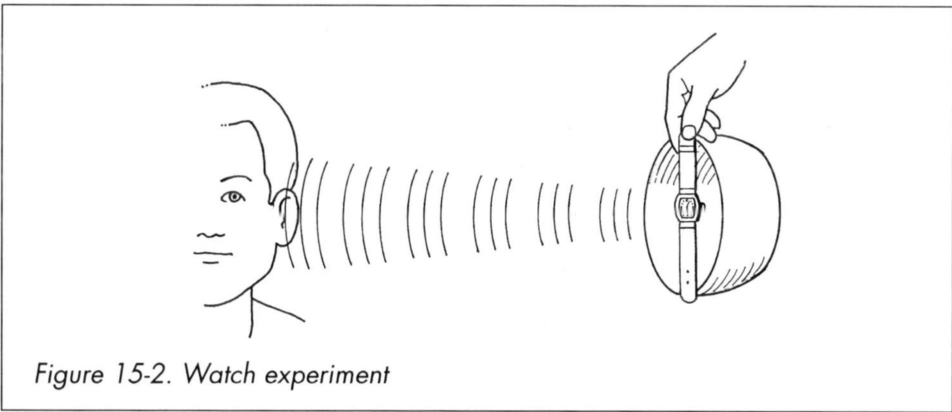

Figure 15-2. Watch experiment

4. Try holding the megaphone to your ear. Can your friend move farther away again so that you can still hear the tick? Sketch the paths of the waves.

5. Set up the two umbrellas as shown (Figure 15-3). Have your friend hold the watch at the focus of one umbrella while you put your ear at the focus of the other. Do you hear the sound of the watch clearly? Explain why. If you sit on the stool, can you hear the sound? Explain.

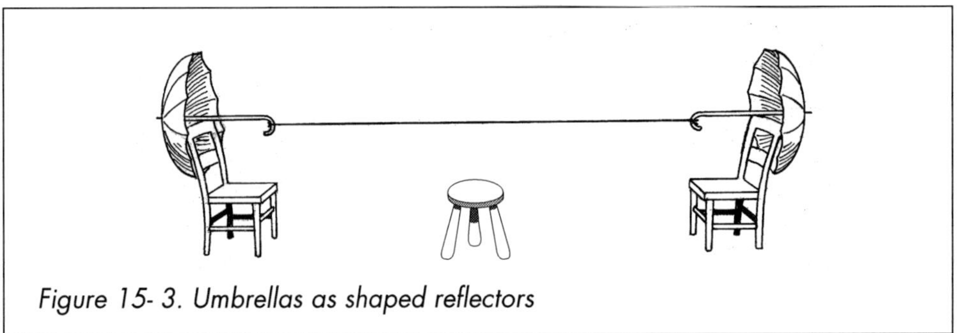

Figure 15- 3. Umbrellas as shaped reflectors

6. Obtain a brightly polished strip of metal from a tin can. Use a comb and sunlight (or projector) to give you parallel rays of light (Figure 15-4). Note the paths taken by the reflected rays as you move and bend the rays in various ways. Try the metal in convex and concave shapes.

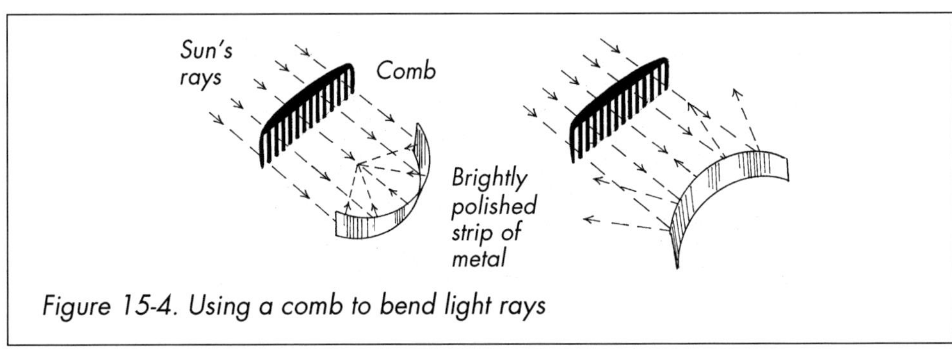

Figure 15-4. Using a comb to bend light rays

16. Surfaces—Bubbles to Spacecraft

An important property of molecules is that there is an attractive force between them. This force depends on the masses of the molecules and their distance from each other. The force decreases as the distance increases. The force holding like molecules together is called cohesion. The force holding unlike molecules together is called adhesion.

In Part B of Figure 16-1, the molecule within the liquid attracts, and is attracted by, all the other molecules around it. We say it is equally attracted on all sides. This is the attractive force of cohesion.

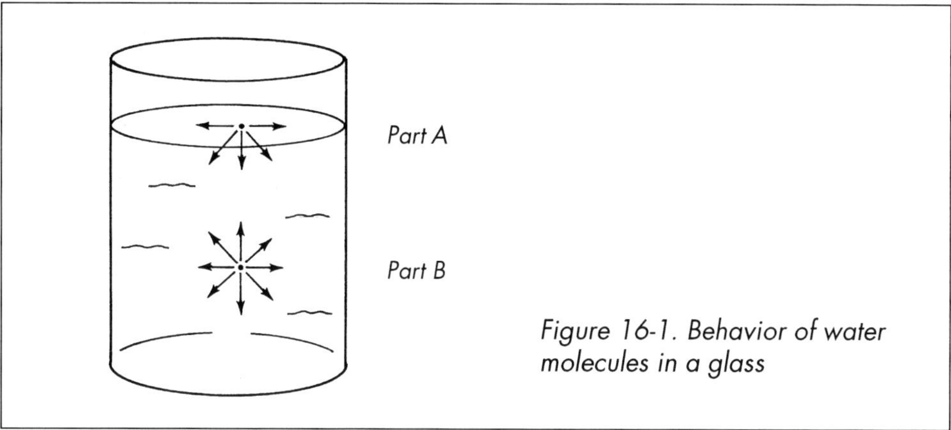

Figure 16-1. Behavior of water molecules in a glass

In Part A, the molecule at the surface is not attracted equally all around. The molecules are actually drawn inward by the attractive force of nearby molecules. Because of the unbalanced nature of the forces acting on the molecules in the surface film, there is strain or tension in the film. The surface force is called surface tension. Many of the important properties of materials depend on the presence of this surface film.

At the edge of the container (Figure 16-2), you will see that the water surface creeps up. For a water molecule near the wall of the container, the force of adhesion is greater than the force of cohesion, so the surface of the water tends to curve upward.

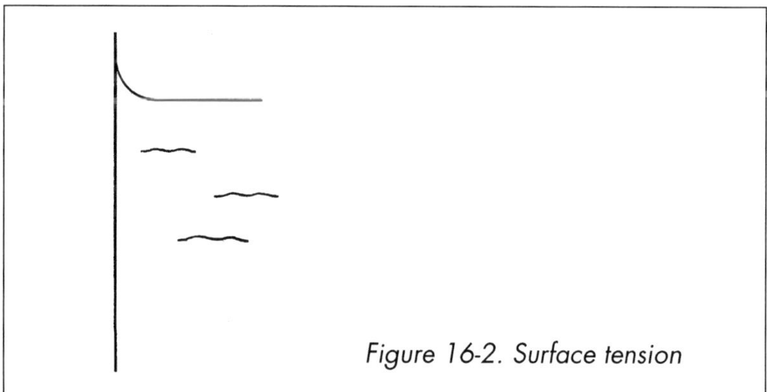

Figure 16-2. Surface tension

Water is home to a wide variety of insects. What enables some insects to walk on its surface? To live underneath without drowning? To go up or down so much more easily than we can, living in air? How do pond skaters of the insect world stay on the surface? What holds them up? A needle or razor blade floats on water. What holds it up? A glass is filled to slightly over-full. What prevents it from overflowing?

All this relates to the idea of a surface film. For example, you can observe how a razor blade indents the surface layer of water. An insect walking on water does the same.

With material surfaces in space, when such surfaces touch, phenomena occur that are not observed in the materials when they are left separated. For example, the metal surfaces of space vehicles docking together would very likely weld one to the other if they were not treated with a separating compound.

Scientists are very interested in the effects of contact between various materials under varying conditions. They research protective layers—wax, paint, thin metal—on exposed surfaces. They learn how to insulate surfaces from contact with each other, from atmospheric factors, space vacuum and intense cold, solar radiation, and other conditions. The properties of surface tension make this possible. Surface tension occurs when molecules in the surface film are subject to forces that do not balance.

Experimenting with Liquid Films

You can demonstrate the properties of liquid films in the following activities.

What you need: natural-bristle paintbrush, glass of water, bowl, vinegar, baking soda, pipe for bubbles, wire loop, wire rectangle, saucer of soapy water, razor blade, dinner plate, needle, waxed paper, pencil

1. Look at the brush. Are the hairs separately visible? Now dip the brush into the glass of water. Describe how the hairs look. Do they cling together or are they still separately visible? Are the hairs wet? Now take the brush out of the water. How are the hairs different? The wet hairs cling together not in the water, but out of the water. Can you explain why? Is a surface film involved (Figure 16-3)?

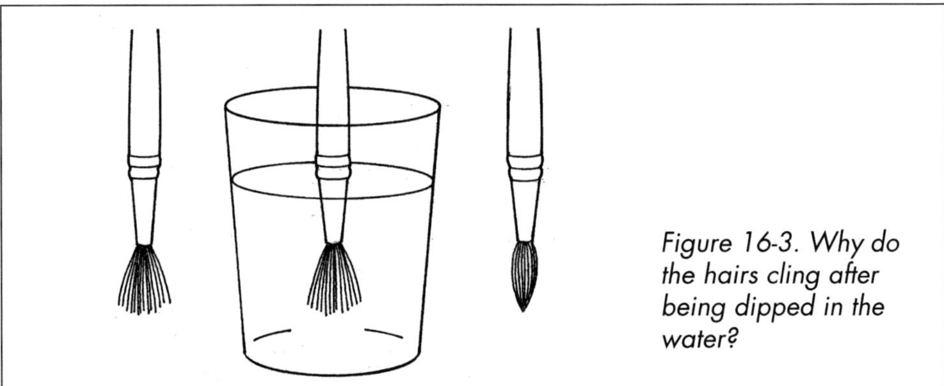

Figure 16-3. Why do the hairs cling after being dipped in the water?

2. Put a little vinegar and soda in the bowl. The heavy gas carbon dioxide forms, but cannot be seen. Now blow a soap bubble and drop it into the bowl. Does it bounce as it strikes the heavy gas, like a rubber ball striking the floor? What does this tell you about the skin of the bubble (Figure 16-4)?

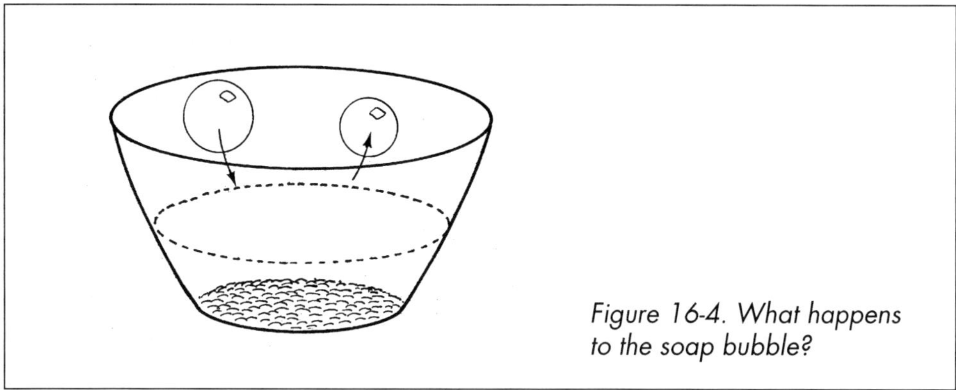

Figure 16-4. What happens to the soap bubble?

3. Place the wire loop below the soapy water surface, then see if you can lift the film out of the water. Try the same with the wire rectangle. Pull the slider and note what the film does. What does this tell you about the film (Figure 16-5)? Try blowing bubbles with the pipe (or straw). How would you describe the bubble film?

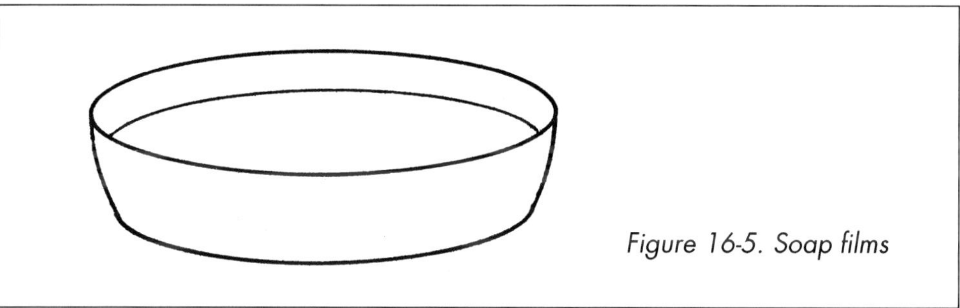

Figure 16-5. Soap films

4. Try floating the razor blade on the water surface in a plate. Does the blade indent the film? Cut a small paper rider, fold it around the needle, and lower it carefully onto the film. Does the needle float ? Does it indent the film (Figure 16-6)?

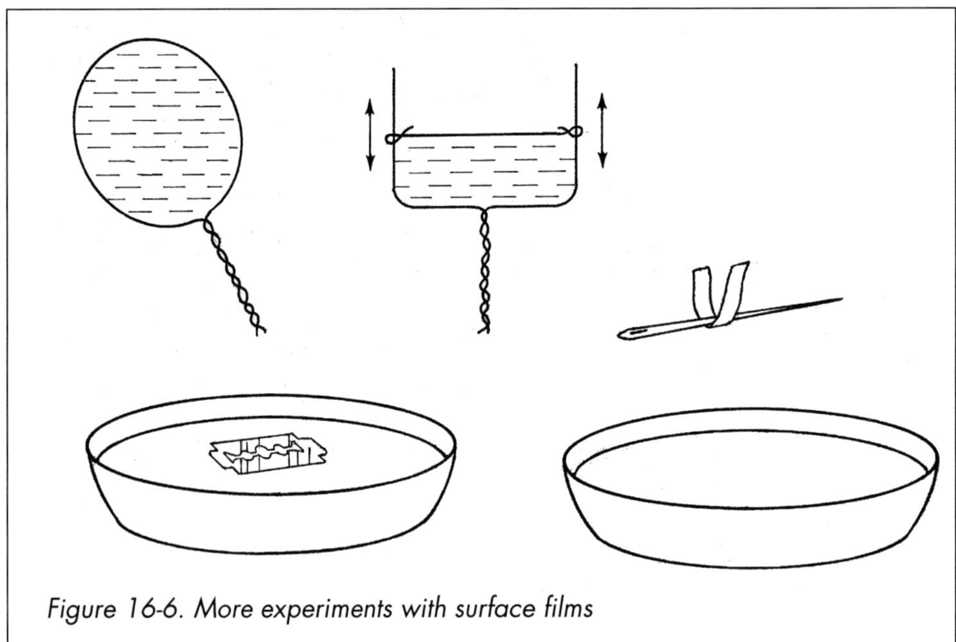

Figure 16-6. More experiments with surface films

5. Shake some water drops, large and small, onto the waxed paper. Are the small drops a different shape from the large ones? Can you explain why? How would you describe the shape of the smaller drops? Why? Poke a drop with the tip of a pencil, then draw the pencil back. Does the drop stretch? Does it try to hold together (Figure 16-7)?

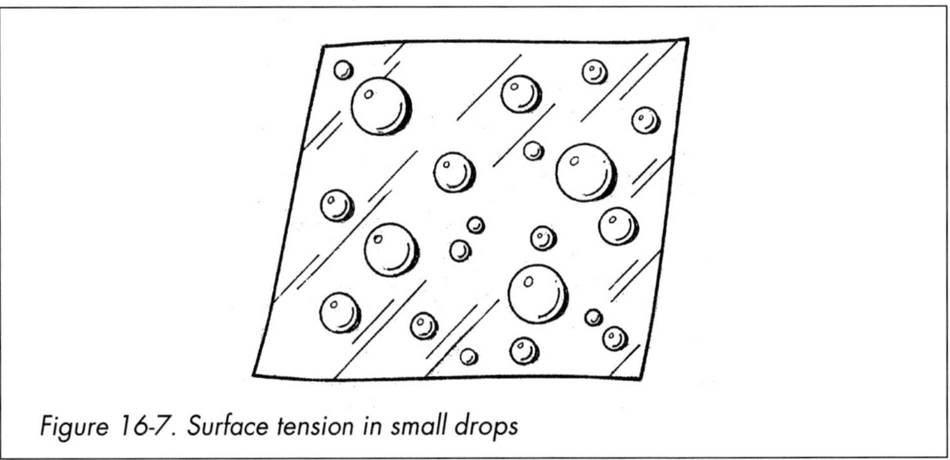

Figure 16-7. Surface tension in small drops

6. Watch small insects walking on the surface of water—pond skaters, springtails, midges, mosquitoes, water spiders. Look through a hand lens to see if they indent the film.

7. Find insects—mosquito wrigglers, soldier fly larvae, and pond snails—that hang from the surface. Look with a lens to find how they hang from the film.

CHAPTER THREE

PROBING THE COSMOS

17. Space Power Sources

Space stations and spacecraft making long journeys need a reliable and efficient source of electrical power to operate onboard electronics such as computers, radio transmitters, television cameras, mechanical equipment, and so on. Thermocouples and solar cells do the job. The thermocouple converts heat energy from the sun or from a nuclear power producer directly into useful electrical energy.

Solar cells make use of the energy in light. When light falls on the surface of materials such as silicon, it sets free electrons from the atoms of the material. Electrons passing along wires form a current and electricity is produced (Photo 5).

Early models of watches with luminous dials contain a small quantity of radium bromide mixed with a fluorescent substance called zinc sulphide. The radium, being radioactive, fires out atomic particles at terrific speed. Every time one of these particles strikes a zinc sulphide molecule, a flash of light results. This makes the watch numbers and hands glow in the dark. While experimenting with uranium, the French scientist Henri Becquerel found that some radiations were strong enough to blacken a photographic plate. Similar energy sources are constructed in space vehicles.

Working with Energy Sources

You may experiment with energy sources for space vehicles.

What you need: small bottle with cork, matches, magnifier, copper and iron wires of same thickness, magnetic compass, coil of many turns of fine wire

Photo 4. The Upper Atmosphere Research satellite (UARS) deploying its solar array panel while in the grasp of the Remote Manipulator System. Solar cells in the panel convert the sun's energy directly into electrical energy to power the electronic systems of the UARS.

1. Make a "magic cannon" by focusing light energy from the sun onto some matches attached to the inside end of a cork in a small bottle (Figure 17-1). Experiment to get the focus right. Describe what happens then. What was the source of the energy that fired the "cannon"? Try to draw the light rays from the sun to the matches.

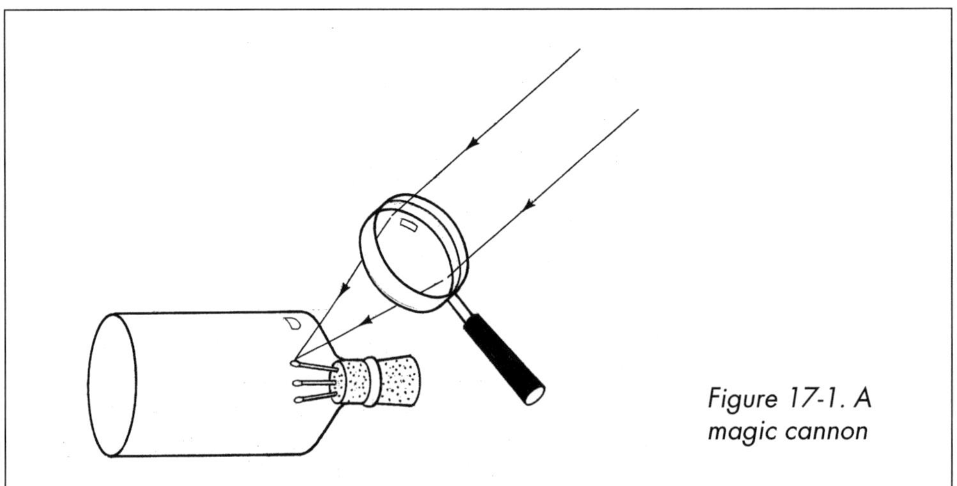

Figure 17-1. A magic cannon

2. Make a simple thermocouple by cleaning the ends of the copper and iron wires, then tightly twisting the ends together. Now heat the twists or junctions at one side

while those at the other side remain cool. Use the wiring shown (Figure 17-2). The compass with the coil of fine insulated wire wound around it acts as a sensitive current detector (galvanometer). The heat produces a flow of electricity that can be measured by the galvanometer. Does the needle of your "galvanometer" deflect or swing? What does this tell you?

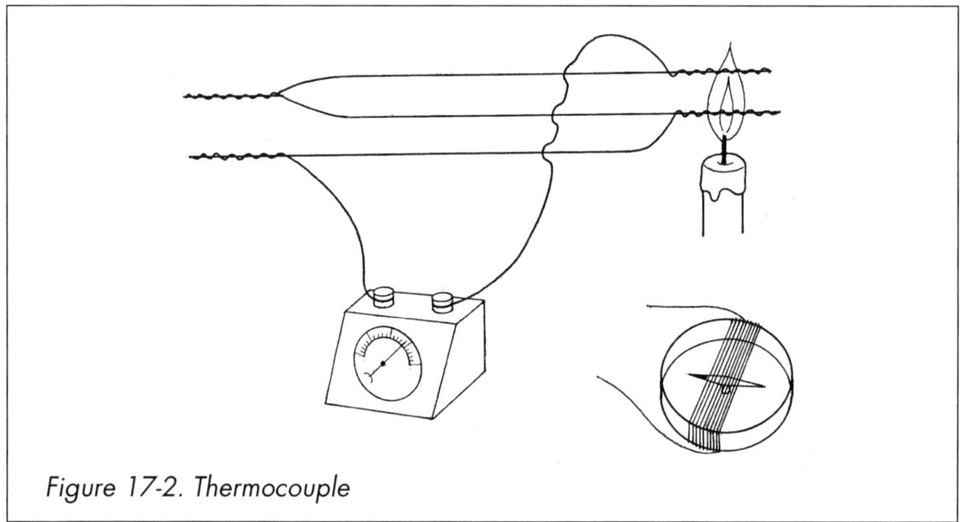

Figure 17-2. Thermocouple

3. As a project, you could try making a working model of a solar-powered car. You would need a model car with an electric motor and gears. The solar power panel of silicon photoelectric cells would be mounted on the roof of the vehicle. Your model could also be fitted with a remote control unit.

18. Radar

Radar stands for <u>ra</u>dio <u>d</u>etection <u>a</u>nd <u>r</u>anging. This is an electronic method for finding the location of and distance to a moving object. In radar, a series of electromagnetic waves or pulses is sent out, and the time needed for the waves to bounce back from the moving object is recorded. Electromagnetic waves travel at the speed of 3×10^8 m/s. A television-like cathode ray tube is used for recording small, exact intervals of time.

Using radar, scientists can tell the speed, altitude, course, and deviations of satellites and separation stages of rockets. Information from radar also tells them about the surface nature of the planets. Radar is used to track meteors and to study the reflecting layers of the ionosphere—the electrified layer above the earth that makes long-distance broadcasting possible. A radio telescope can make contact with the moon. It takes the pulse of radar waves 2.5 seconds to make the round trip to the moon and back again—a distance of some 800,000 km. Scientists obtain valuable information about conditions in the ionosphere in this way.

Looking at Wave Action

You can find out how radar works by experimenting with a ripple tank, then using a soft rubber ball.

What you need: commercial ripple tank or tray with a raised edge, water, pencil, brick (to act as test object), soft rubber or foam plastic ball, 50-cm rubber strand or rubber bands looped together, leaves, cushion, plastic bucket, tray of earth, etc.

1. Pour water into the tray to a depth of 1–2 cm. Make waves by vibrating the water with a pencil. Note: If you use a glass tray, having a lamp above it better enables you to see the waves on a white paper screen placed underneath the tray. Describe how the waves travel. What happens when they strike the edge of the tray? If you use a round, dark-colored tray, vibrate the water at the center. How do the waves travel? What happens when they strike the edge (Figure 18-1)?

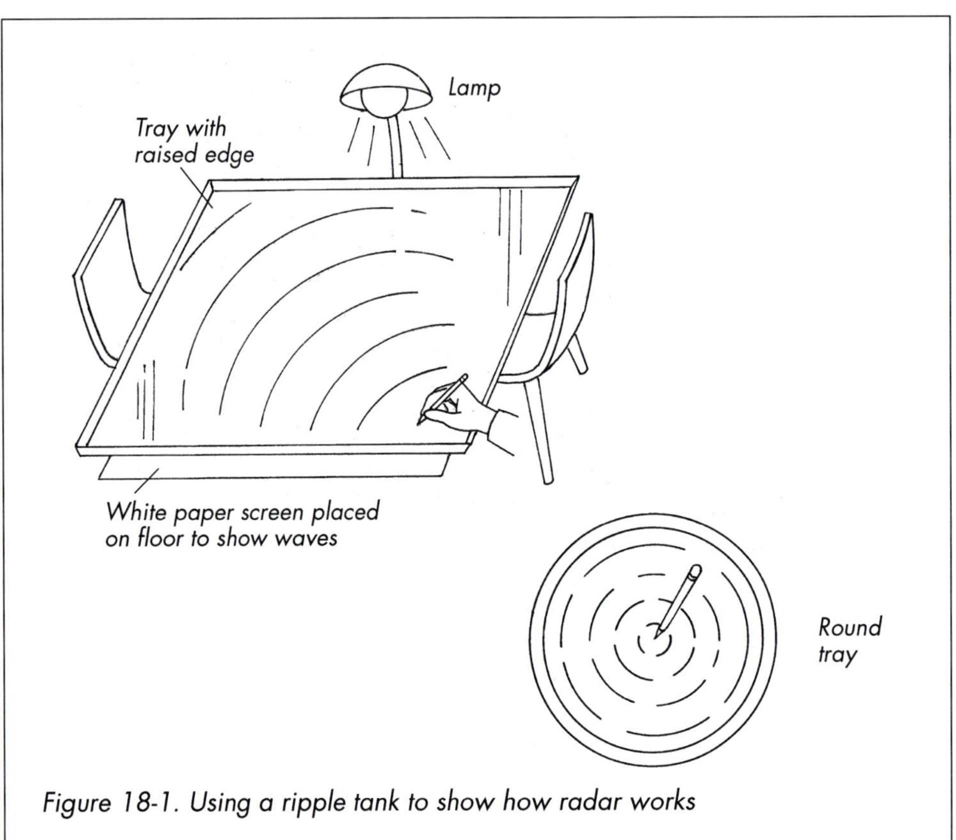

Figure 18-1. Using a ripple tank to show how radar works

2. Place a stone to act as a test object in the tray. Vibrate the water as before. How do the waves behave when they strike the test object? Draw a sketch. How is this like the waves of radar (Figure 18-2)?

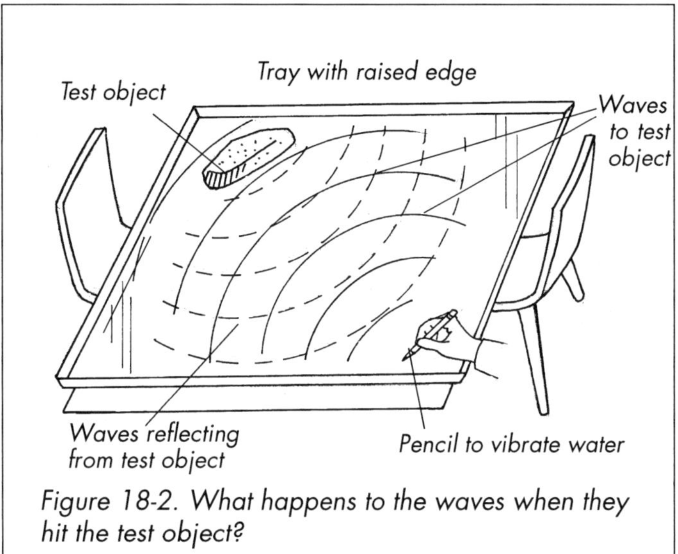

Figure 18-2. What happens to the waves when they hit the test object?

3. Tie the soft rubber (or foam plastic) ball to the end of the 50 cm rubber strand. Have your eyes closed or be blindfolded. Have a partner arrange various test objects around you. Take the free end of the rubber strand and toss the ball in all directions from you (Figure 18-3). Can you tell hard surfaces from soft? By repeatedly bouncing the ball from an object, can you tell about its shape? Can you describe the location of different objects? Find out if radar waves would work like this.

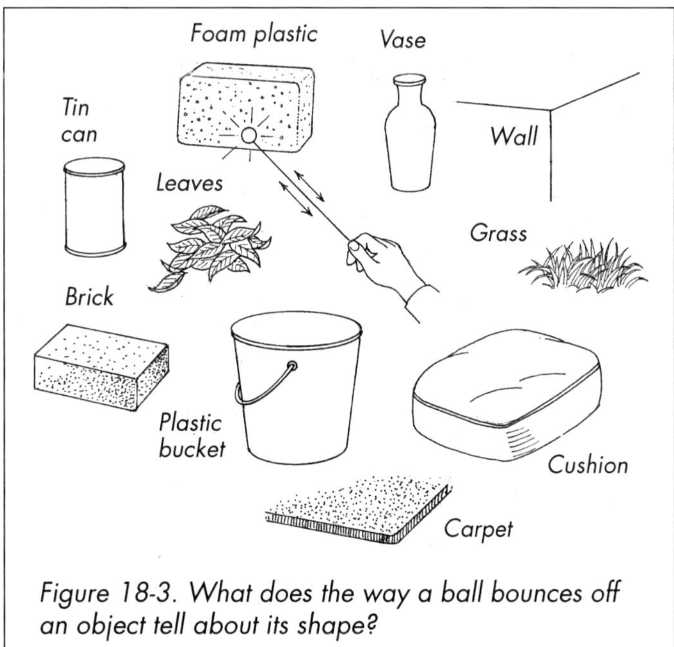

Figure 18-3. What does the way a ball bounces off an object tell about its shape?

4. An Italian named Marconi was the first person to send radio waves across the Atlantic. Write a paragraph on how Marconi set about doing this.

5. How is radar used to explore:
    a. the moon?
    b. the planets?
    c. the ionosphere?

19. Tracking with Doppler

When you are out riding in a car, the horn sounds the same no matter what speed you are traveling. But when you stand on the side of the street, the horn of a fast-moving car has a different tone. It sounds with a higher pitch as the car approaches you and with a lower pitch as the car goes away from you. This is known as the Doppler effect. As the car speeds toward you, the sound waves reach your ear more frequently than they do when the car stands still. This gives a rise in pitch. The sound waves reach your ear less frequently as the car speeds away from you. This gives a drop in pitch.

Rockets and spacecraft are tracked as they hurtle through space. One method, an all-electric radio wave signal, is known as DOVAP. That stands for <u>DO</u>ppler <u>V</u>elocity <u>A</u>nd <u>P</u>osition. Simple to operate and very reliable, it makes use of the Doppler effect. Just as the car horn rises as the car approaches and falls as it goes by, radio signals from a rocket or spacecraft increase in frequency on moving toward a receiver on earth and drop in frequency as the craft moves away.

Using this method it is possible to plot the course taken by the rocket or spacecraft and to measure its speed and distance during flight.

Studying the Doppler Effect

You can demonstrate how the Doppler effect works.

What you need: fine wire (about 30 gauge), cardboard tube or broom handle, whistle, rubber or plastic tubing

1. Wind about 20 turns of the fine wire around the broom handle, keeping the spacing even. Slip the coil off the handle and place it on the table. The evenly spaced turns of the coil will represent waves. Have an observer stand at "A." Holding the coil by its last turn, move it slowly and evenly toward the observer (Figure 19-1). What happens to the "waves" (the turns of the coil)? Do they tend to bunch up? What happens to the frequency of the wave? Is it greater or less?

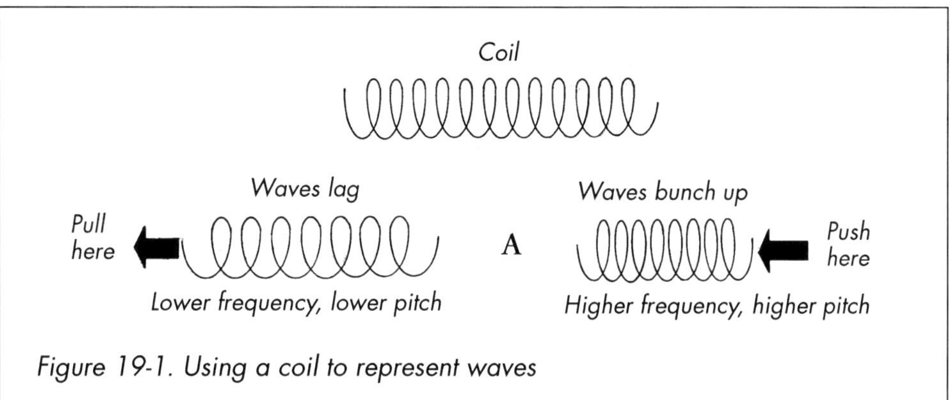

Figure 19-1. Using a coil to represent waves

When the coil is opposite the observer, take it by the front turn and move it slowly and evenly as before, away from "A." What happens to the turns of the coil (the "waves") this time? Do they tend to lag behind one another a little? What can you say about the frequency of the wave? Is it greater or less?

Write a few sentences telling how this demonstrates the Doppler effect.

2. Fit the mouth of the whistle into one end of the rubber or plastic tubing. With your friends standing 4–5 meters in front of you, blow through the other end of the tube so they hear the true pitch of the note given out by the whistle. Then, still blowing into the whistle, swing the tubing in a large circle above your head (Figure 19-2). How does the pitch change as the whistle moves toward your friends? How does the pitch change as it moves away from them? In terms of waves, how do you explain this seeming change in pitch?

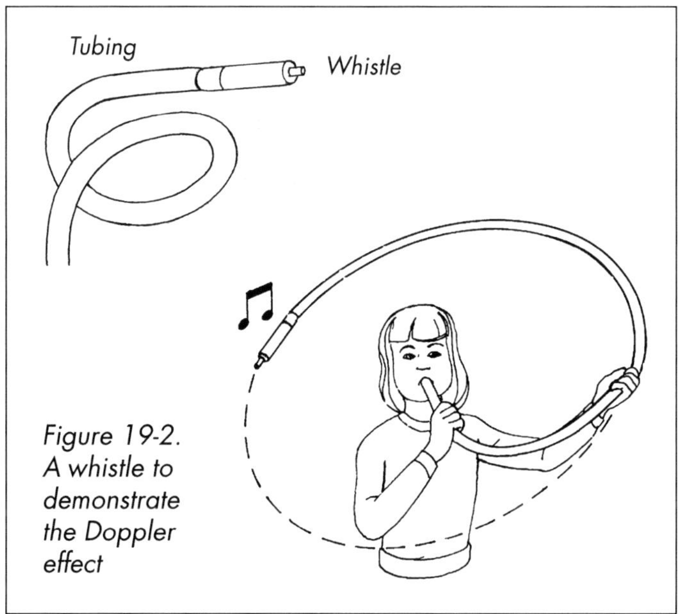

Figure 19-2. A whistle to demonstrate the Doppler effect

3. Find out more about how the Doppler effect is important and useful to astronomers.

20. Crystals

The beauty of a crystal, whether it be a sparkling ruby, a sapphire, a diamond, or a humble snowflake, never ceases to attract us. Just as fascinating and beautiful is the inner structure—how the particles of the crystal are arranged, how the crystal grows to what it is.

Crystals grow from a cluster of molecules or atoms of the substance. Particles of matter attach themselves in orderly fashion to the center, which increases in size. The smallest part of the crystal that shows all the features of the substance and decides the final crystal shape is called the unit cell. Many crystals found in nature do not have perfect shapes but are modified, as though their opposite corners are cut off.

Mercury iodide crystals have possible uses as sensitive X-ray and gamma-ray detectors. The crystals have special electrical properties and can work at room temperatures rather than at the very low temperatures needed by other substances. The crystals could be used in portable detector devices for nuclear power plant monitoring, for prospecting, in medicine, and in astronomy.

Crystals of mercury iodide grown on earth have defects: they grow unevenly, are fragile, and deform under their own weight. But in the low gravity of the space shuttle lab, scientists can make large single crystals with few defects. Tests have showed that crystals grown in space are superior to those grown on earth (Photo 6).

Photo 5. These samples of insulin were grown in space for NASA's Protein Crystal Growth experiment.

Making Crystal Models

You can make crystal models.

What you need: crystal samples, copies of crystal shape templates, card stock sheets

1. Look at some crystal samples through a hand lens. Describe the crystal shapes. Make sketches.

2. Make models of crystals by following the instructions on the sheets of diagrams (Figures 20-1 through 20-4).

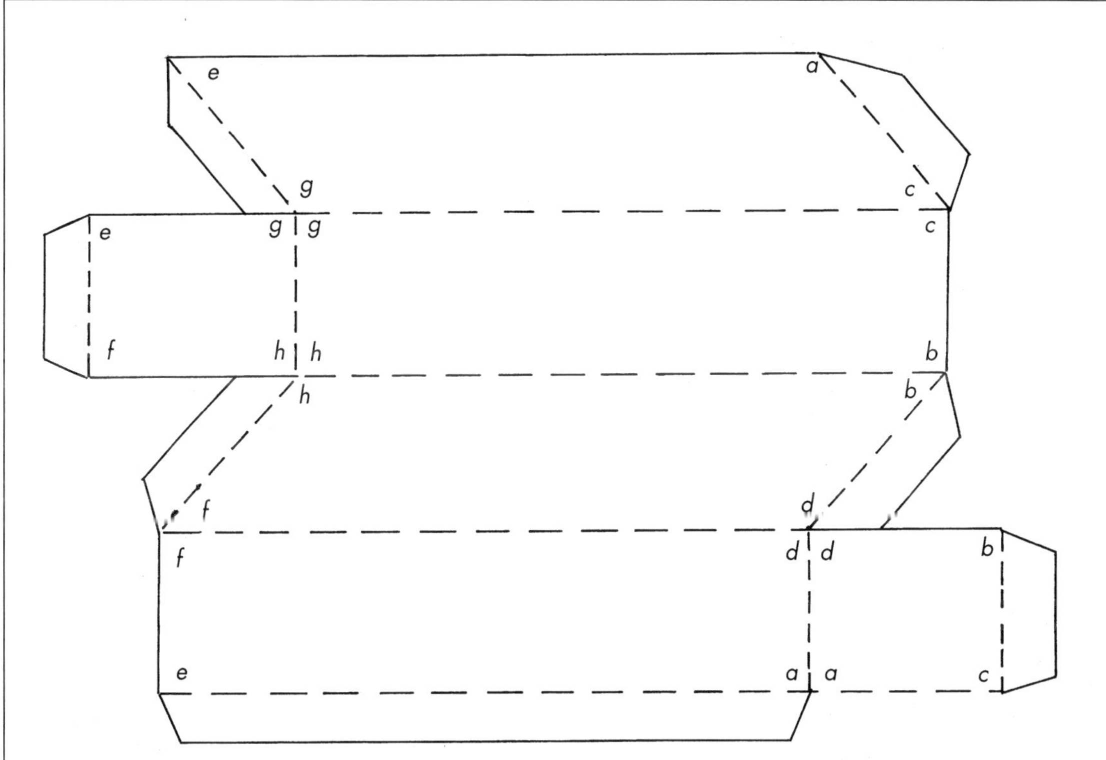

Figure 20-1. Monoclinic system crystal shape: Paste on thin cardboard. Cut on all solid lines. Be sure to cut into corners ggg, hhh, and ddd. Fold on dotted lines. Paste tabs to undersides of edges with corresponding letters.

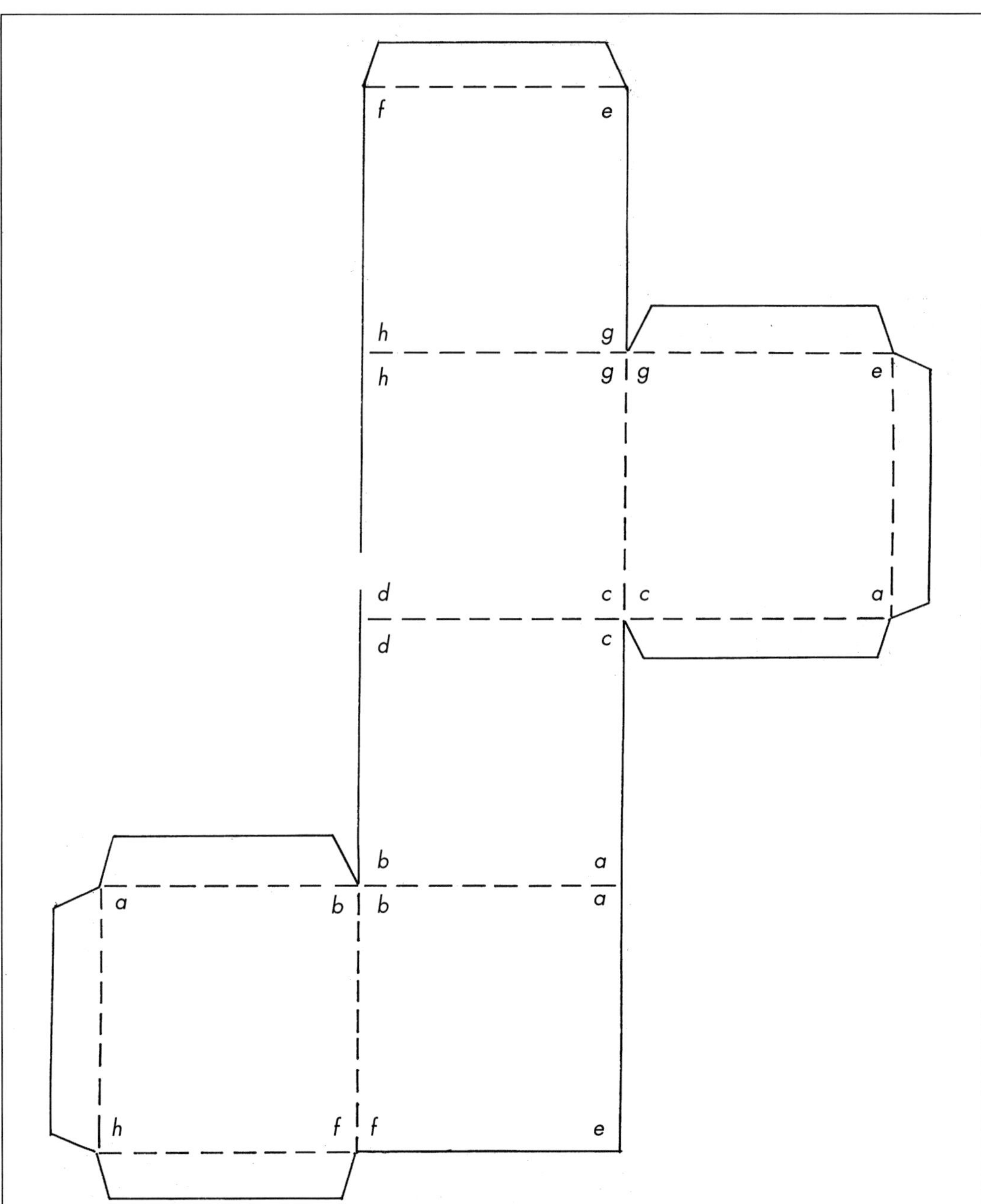

Figure 20-2. Cubic crystal shape: Paste on thin cardboard. Cut on all solid lines. Fold on dotted lines. Paste tabs to undersides of edges with corresponding letters.

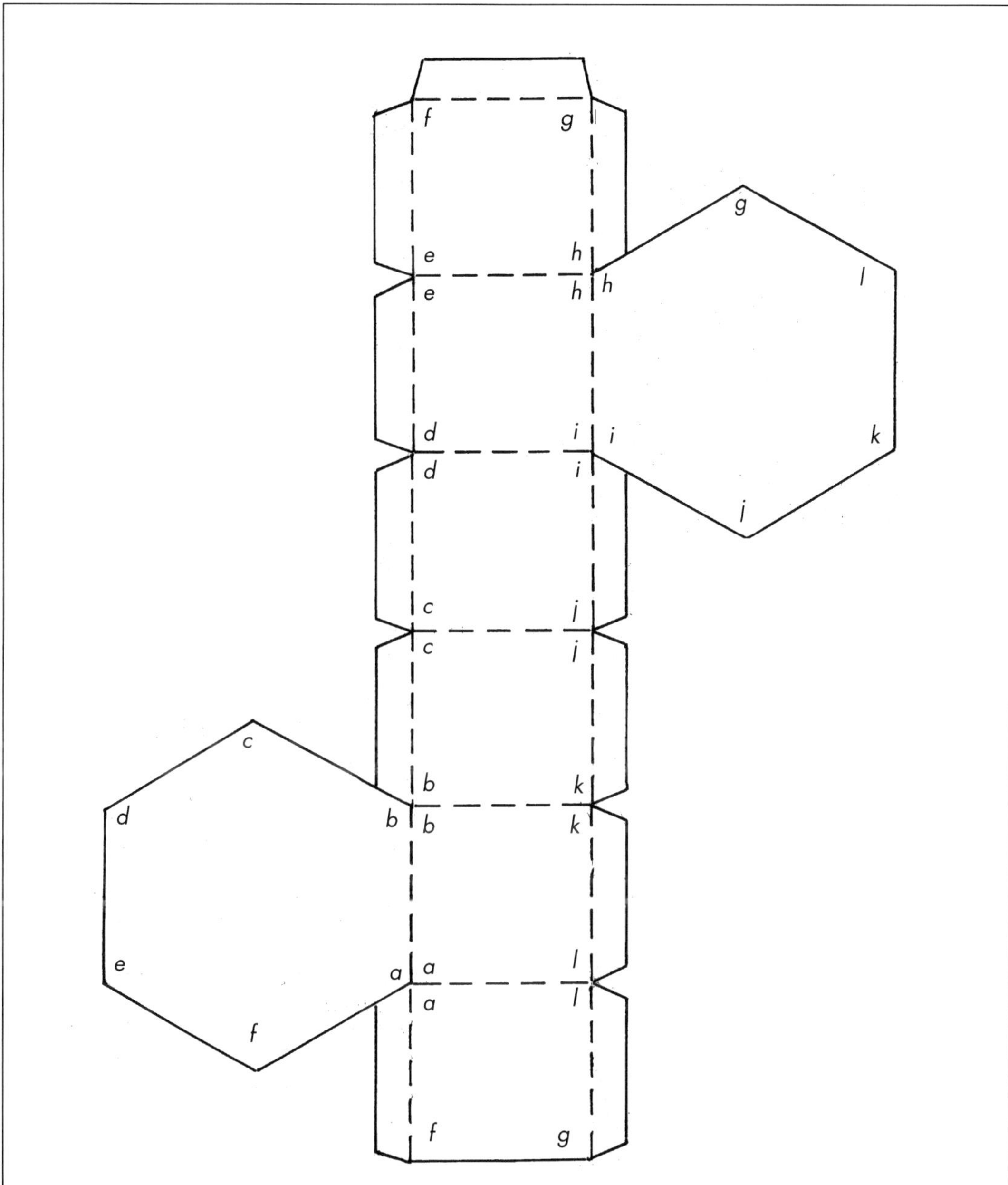

Figure 20-3. Hexagon crystal shape: Paste on light cardboard. Cut on all solid lines. Be sure to cut into corners hhh, iii, bbb, and aaa. Fold on dotted lines. Paste tabs to undersides of edges with corresponding letters.

Name ______________________ Date ______________

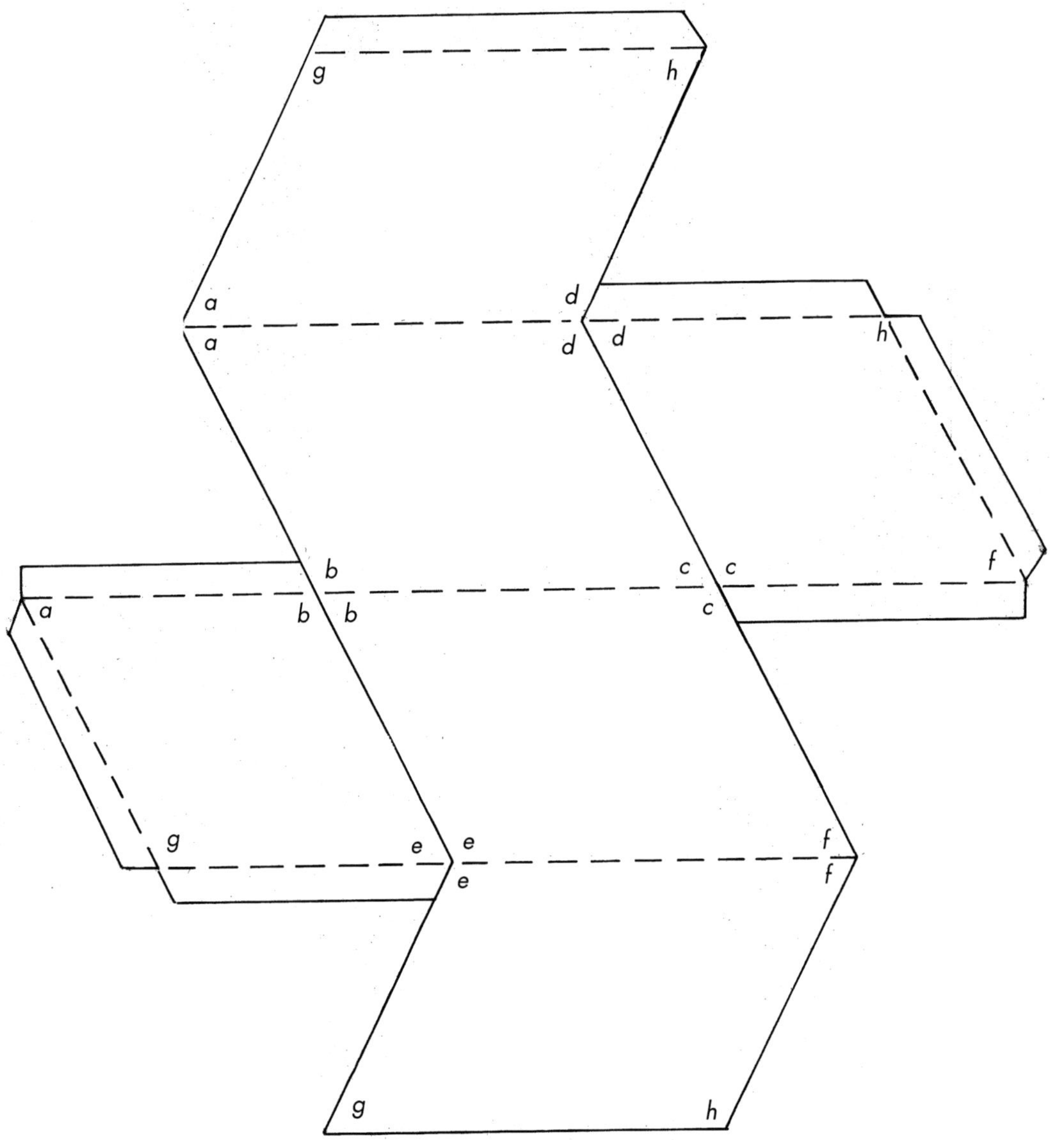

Figure 20-4. Triclinic crystal shape: Paste on light cardboard. Cut on all solid lines. Fold on dotted lines. Paste tabs to undersides of edges with corresponding letters.

3. Liquid crystals are a form of matter in between solids and liquids. Find out what you can about liquid crystals.

4. Make a display of your crystal models.

21. Imaging the Earth

Landsats are satellites that study earth's resources such as minerals, forests, crops, and life in the sea. The satellites also find out how pollution of our atmosphere and oceans is affecting earth.

U.S. Landsats orbit the earth at a height of about 700 kilometers. They take images of the earth using a scanning device. An oscillating mirror records details on the earth's surface in strips 185 kilometers square. The scanning is done in light of several wavelengths, including green and red visible light and four infrared wavelengths.

Information may be sent directly to a ground receiving station or to a Comsat (communications satellite). Images assist engineers in the design and construction of roads, bridges, and railways. The satellites can also tell how good crops are and can pick out areas of disease. Images show where trees need to be planted in forests. Forest fires are reported right away.

Images of the sea tell where there are schools of fish. Landsats also report on ocean currents to assist ships in planning their courses.

Important mineral discoveries made by Landsats include oil in the Sudan, tin in Brazil, and uranium in Australia.

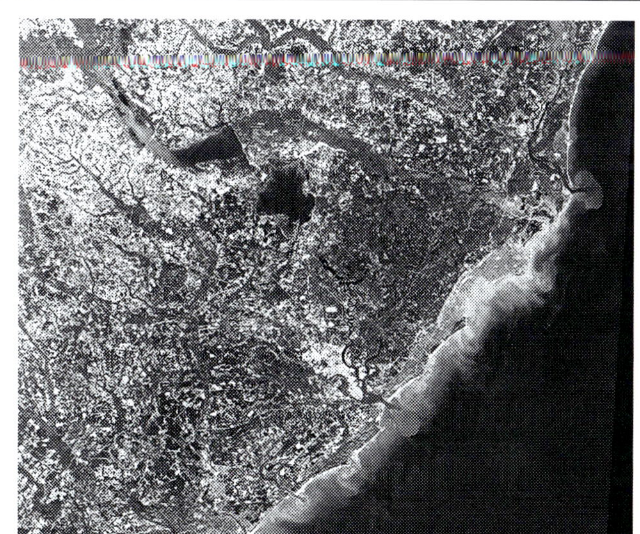

Photo 6. Landsat 4 took these images of the South Carolina coast, shown here in "true" colors. In these images, you can see how sediments along the shore are stirred up by waves, and how patterns of off-shore siltation are shaped by muddy river water flowing into the ocean.

"Prospecting" with a Magnetometer

You can make a simple magnetometer and "prospect" for "minerals."

What you need: two sewing needles, magnet, 5 × 2.5-cm card, thread, plastic plate or dish, sheet of cardboard, pebbles, iron washers, nuts and bolts

A magnetometer is used in the air and at sea to locate mineral deposits. The heart of the magnetometer is a magnet, finely balanced, that detects changes in the pattern of the earth's magnetic field due to mineral deposits such as iron ore in the earth's crust.

1. Place the various pebbles, nuts and bolts, and washers in the dish and cover it with a sheet of cardboard. Make the magnetometer by folding the card in half. Then magnetize the two needles by stroking about 30 times in one direction only with a strong magnet. Next, insert the needles in the card as shown, like poles opposite each other (Figure 21-1). Suspend the card by a thread. Does it move back and forth? In which direction does it finally come to rest?

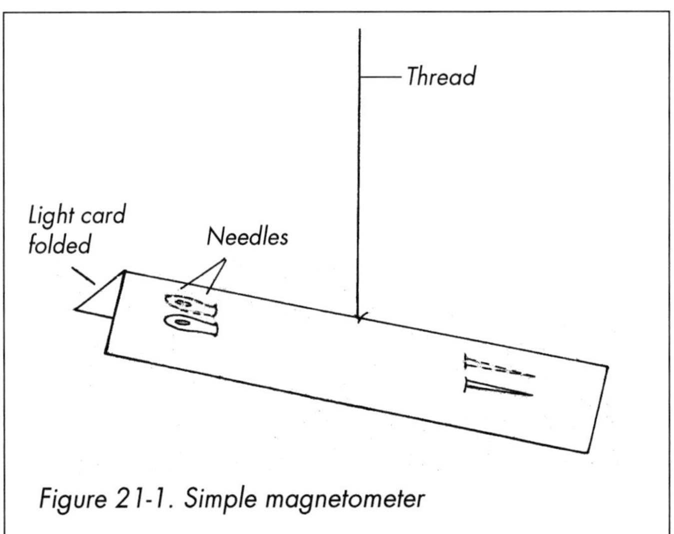

Figure 21-1. Simple magnetometer

2. To "prospect," bring the magnetometer down to about 1 cm above the dish. Move it backward and forward in a regular way so that you get a complete "survey" of the dish, which represents part of the earth's crust. What happens when the magnetometer passes over an iron "deposit"? Put a check mark on the dish wherever a deposit occurs. When you have finished, lift the cardboard cover and see how good your prospecting was. Now move the deposits around and let a friend have a try. If you have problems getting the magnetometer to dip, try substituting a small piece of magnet for one of the iron deposits. Does this give you a good result?

22. What Is Light? (Part 1)

> *I have also a paper afloat containing an electromagnetic*
> *theory of light, which till I am convinced to the contrary*
> *I hold to be great guns.*
>
> —James Clerk Maxwell *(1831–79)*

In the middle of the seventeenth century, Sir Isaac Newton put forward the particle theory of light. In this theory, light consisted of a stream of particles—corpuscles, Newton called them. When the "corpuscles" entered the eye, they gave the sensation of light. Then, between 1812 and 1818, A.J. Fresnel (France) and Thomas Young (England) performed experiments that showed that light had wavelike properties.

More theories and discoveries about light followed. Olaf Roemer, a Danish astronomer, by observing the moons of Jupiter, worked out the velocity of light. Armand Fizeau, the French scientist, also measured the velocity with great accuracy, his figure being 3.15×10^8 meters per second (186,000 miles per second). In 1873, a Scot, James Clerk Maxwell, showed that an electromagnetic wave travels away from a vibrating electric charge at the speed of light. The wave was made up of electrical and magnetic fields. Twenty years later, Heinrich Hertz of Germany demonstrated electromagnetic waves in an experiment and showed that the waves possessed many of the properties of light.

It was also discovered that when light of sufficiently high frequency falls on a metal surface, electrons are ejected from the surface. This effect, the photoelectric effect (used in a camera's light meter), was explained in 1905 by Albert Einstein. The light energy, instead of being distributed through space in the fields of electromagnetic waves, was concentrated in small packets or particles called photons. This seems to support Newton's corpuscular theory. Light, then, has the properties of both waves and particles. We use the electromagnetic theory to explain how light from the sun and stars travels through space. The ways in which light interacts with matter are best explained by the particle theory.

Photo 7. Light streams from the outermost part of the sun's atmosphere—the corona.

The Behavior of Light

You can investigate some of the properties of light.

What you need: Ping-Pong ball, mirror, glass of water, pencil, match, saucer, magnifying glass, large tray of water or paddling pool, fresh soapy water, cup

1. Reflection: Throw the Ping-Pong ball at the floor or wall at an angle and note the angle at which the ball bounces back. How do the two angles compare (Figure 22-1)?

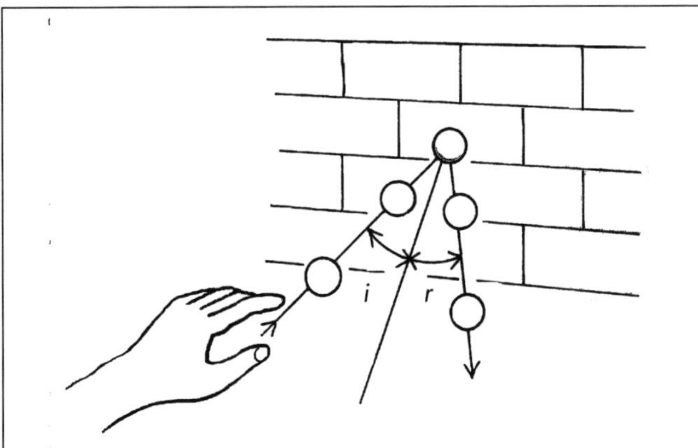

Figure 22-1. The angle at which the ball strikes the wall (angle of incidence, i) is equal to the angle it bounces off (angle of reflection, r).

2. Hold the mirror so that it reflects a beam of light across the room. Note carefully the angles of incidence and reflection. These are the angles measured from the normal, an imaginary line drawn perpendicular to the plane of the mirror (Figure 22-2). Can you now state an important law about the reflection of light?

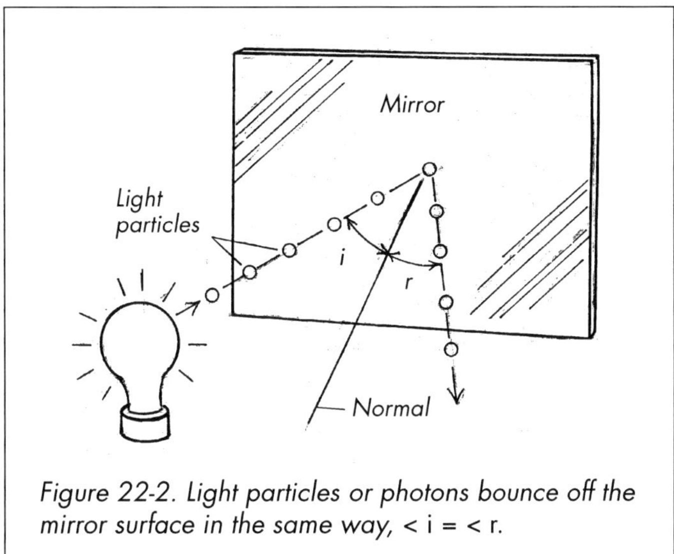

Figure 22-2. Light particles or photons bounce off the mirror surface in the same way, < i = < r.

3. Refraction: Take the glass of water and place the pencil in it. Look at the pencil from the side of the glass. Describe how it looks. Does it look bent? Explain why (Figure 22-3).

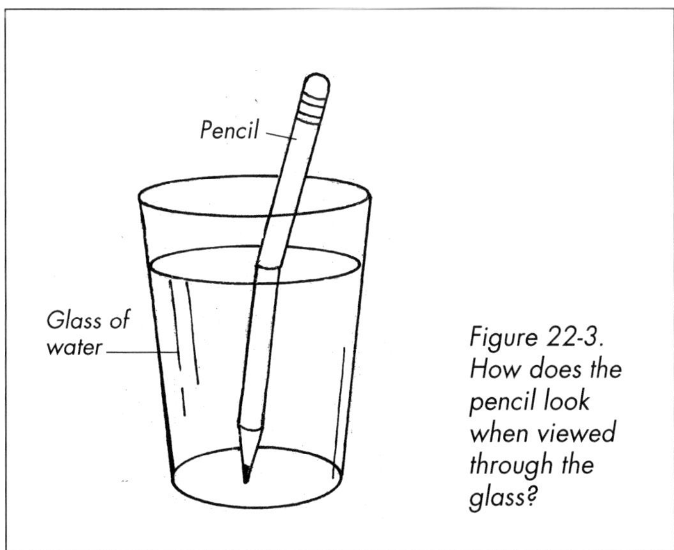

Figure 22-3. How does the pencil look when viewed through the glass?

4. Go outside and focus strong sunlight on a match-head in a saucer. What happens? What does the magnifying glass do to the sun's rays? What is meant by "refraction of light" (Figure 22-4)?

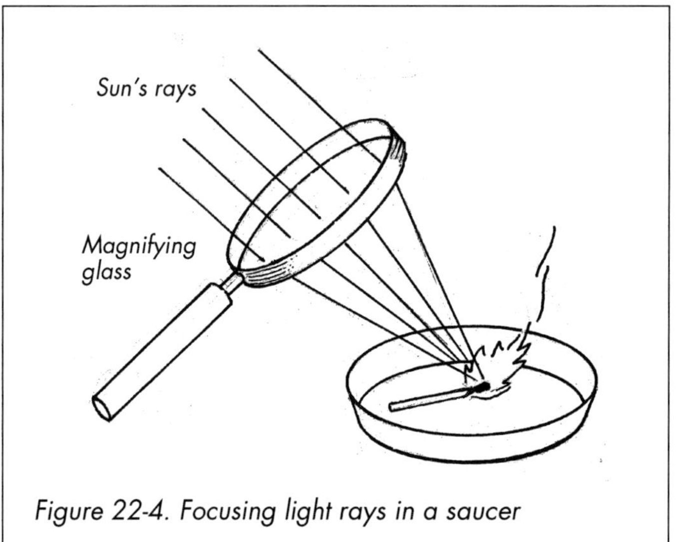

Figure 22-4. Focusing light rays in a saucer

5. Waves: Tap the surface of the water in a tray or paddling pool with a pencil at a steady rate (Figure 22-5). Describe how the waves spread out. Find names for the top of the wave, the base, and the crest-to-crest distance. What is meant by the "frequency" of the wave? Try demonstrating frequency with your paddling pool.

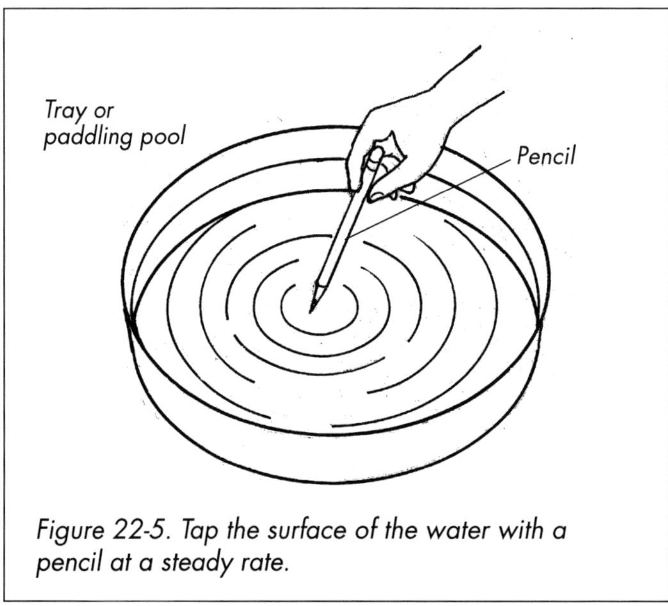

Figure 22-5. Tap the surface of the water with a pencil at a steady rate.

6. Interference: Dip the open end of a cup in fresh soapy water until a soap film covers it. Look at the top of the soap film in strong light (Figure 22-6). Look for red

and blue bands spread from the top down. Do the color patterns change or stay the same? The soap film has two skins or surfaces, inner and outer, with a layer of water sandwiched in between. Light waves reflect from each surface. When the two waves are in step, the color will be brighter, because each reflected wave strengthens the effect of the other. But when the two waves are out of step, they interfere, and this color is destroyed. Light waves not destroyed are colors left over; these are the colors you see. Because the film changes in thickness all the time due to the water layer, the colors change all the time. The eye sees a beautiful play of colors (Figure 22-7). The interference of light is sometimes referred to as "lost light." Explain how light is lost in your experiment. Write a few sentences and include diagrams with your answer.

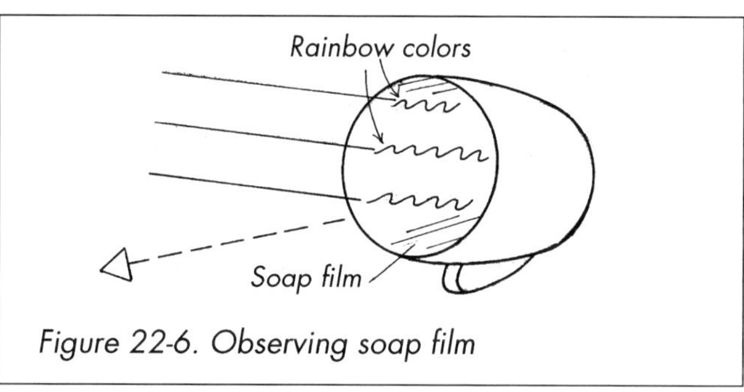

Figure 22-6. Observing soap film

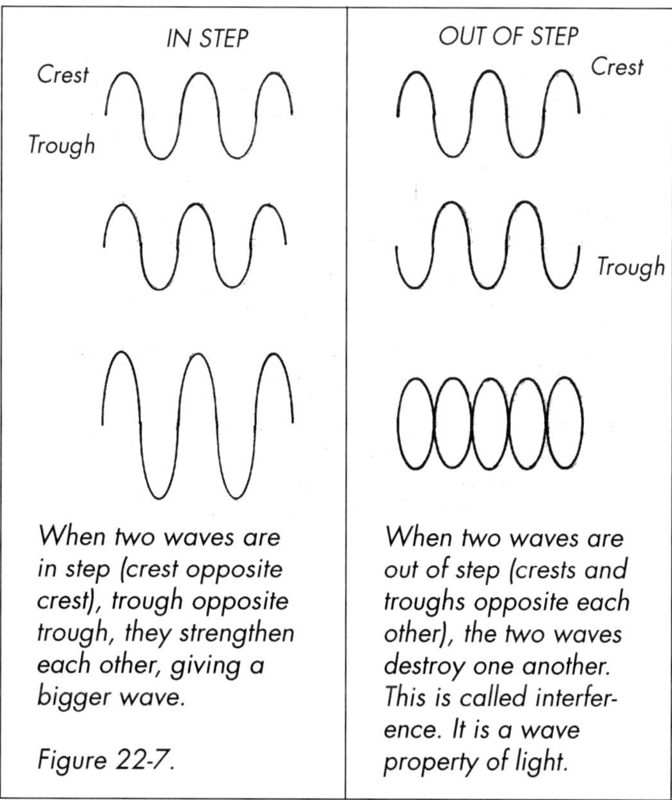

When two waves are in step (crest opposite crest), trough opposite trough, they strengthen each other, giving a bigger wave.

Figure 22-7.

When two waves are out of step (crests and troughs opposite each other), the two waves destroy one another. This is called interference. It is a wave property of light.

23. What Is Light? (Part 2)

One of the most beautiful sights often seen on a slightly hazy day is a series of colored rings around the sun or moon. The rings, called coronae, are a diffraction effect: They are seen within five or six diameters at most from either sun or moon.

Observing Diffraction

What you need: clear plastic, talcum powder, lamp, flashlight, black paper, basin of water, small mirror, pieces of colored cellophane

1. You can show how diffraction works by forming coronae around a distant light source. First rub the piece of clear plastic with a cloth to charge it with static electricity. Now give the plastic a *light* dusting of talcum powder (or similar powder). In a darkened room, hold the plastic in front of your eyes and look through the dust film at a bare electric light about six meters away. How many sets of coronae do you see around the bare light? How many colors can you pick out? What color is on the outside of each corona? Name other colors you can recognize. For best results in this experiment, use a point source of light. You can get this by covering the reflector of a flashlight with black paper, leaving only the bulb exposed. Find out how the dust particles form coronae. Write 3–4 sentences.

   Next time you stand on a wharf or jetty, watch the waves as they strike a pier, sidle around and go on their way, bending into the space that ought to be the shadow of the object. Water waves, sound waves, light waves, and even earthquake waves show this property of wave diffraction.

2. Spectrum: To obtain a rainbow spectrum, fill a basin with water and lean a small mirror against the inside, making sure it is completely covered with water. Allow sunlight to fall on the mirror. Now look at the reflected rays on the wall (Figure 23-1). What shows on the wall? Name the colors in order. Disturb the water with your finger for a minute. What happens to the colors? When the water settles, what do you see? Hold a sheet of red cellophane over the spectrum. What shows on the wall? Repeat with sheets of other colors. What colors show on the wall? Record your results. Record also which colors are subtracted. What is the definition of an absorption spectrum?

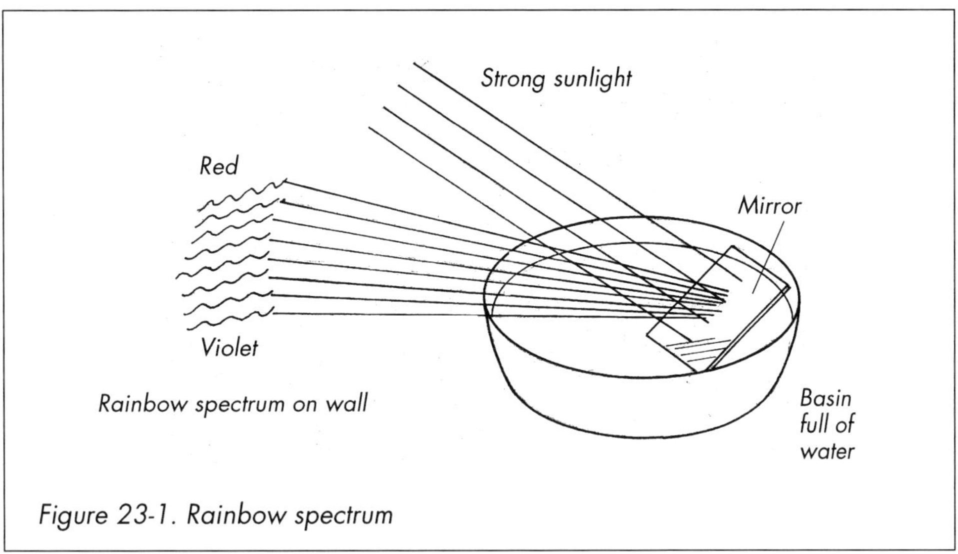

Figure 23-1. Rainbow spectrum

3. Find a copy of the poem "The Torch Bearers" by Alfred Noyes. Read to your class about how Newton discovered the spectrum.

4. How have your experiments helped you to answer the title question, "What Is Light?" Write a paragraph. Include notes on how light is important both to the growing plant and to the astronomer.

5. Find out what you can about the JCMT—the James Clerk Maxwell Telescope.

24. IRAS—Infrared Astronomy Satellite

Infrared radiation has wavelengths longer than red light. The human eye cannot see it. In the spectrum, infrared reaches up to radio wavelengths. Infrared is thermal (heat) radiation coming from any body with a temperature above absolute zero. In January 1983, an 810-kilogram spacecraft called IRAS (Figure 24-1) carried the first infrared telescope into space. Its task was to map the heat of the cosmos.

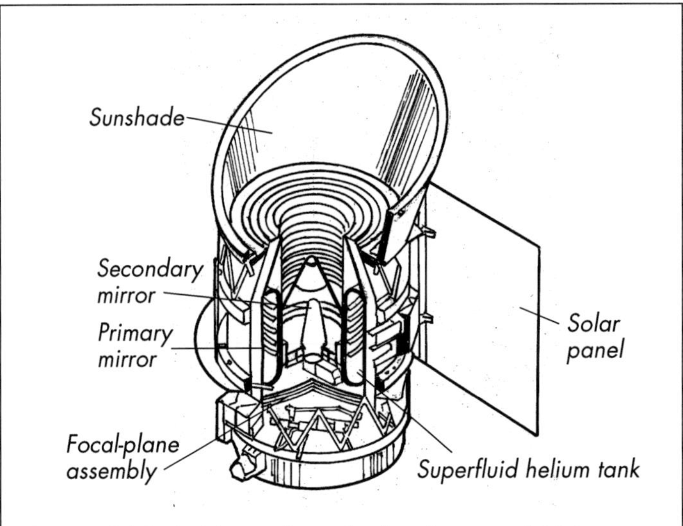

Figure 24-1. IRAS was launched in January 1983 into a near-polar orbit and was designed to make an all-sky infrared survey. It revealed active star-forming regions in the great Magellanic Cloud, the nearest galaxy to ours.

IRAS made a survey of the entire sky, giving astronomers a fuller picture of the universe. It showed what lies beyond clouds of dust and gas that hide much of the universe from Earth.

The delicate detectors on IRAS were chilled in liquid helium at –271° C (about absolute zero) while the satellite searched out energy sources emitting infrared rays. The sky maps and catalogues from IRAS findings list as many as one million infrared energy sources.

Like IRAS, you can have a temperature hunt and make a temperature map.

Make a Temperature Map

What you need: thermometer, pad, pencil

1. Listen in as the radio or TV weather forecaster states the temperature for the day, telephone the weather office, or look in the newspaper. Find out how these sources get their readings.

2. Make a list of places you think could be explored to see how they compare with the given temperature range for the day. Try these and any others you can think of: outdoors in direct sunlight, in the shade of a tree, on the sunny side of a hedge, on the shady side of a bush, on the grass of a lawn, against a sunny wall, 5 cm above the lawn, 15–30 cm below lawn surface (make a hole with a stick), on a north

slope, on a south slope, on a concrete path, 15 cm above a concrete path, in wet soil, in dry soil, under a rock, in the shade of a tall building, in a stream or pond, indoors in various places.

3. Plot your results in graph form and explain the differences. Then list the places showing the highest and lowest temperatures, and those places with the same temperature as that of the forecaster you consulted.

4. Make a temperature map of the grounds where you took your readings.

5. Rattlesnakes on the hunt for prey detect infrared radiation very well. Find out how they are able to do this.

6. What was Galileo's thermoscope?

25. The Mysterious Rays

What are cosmic rays? Where do they come from? What tremendous forces far out in space are at work producing them? These are some of the questions cosmic ray scientists are trying to answer about these mysterious particles that continually bombard our earth.

Cosmic rays are atomic particles of very high energy. They are mainly charged hydrogen atoms traveling with speeds approaching that of light. Some cosmic ray particles have enormous energies far above any produced by our atom-smashing machines. Will humans ever succeed in harnessing this vast storehouse of energy, putting it to practical use?

Scientists know there are different types of cosmic rays. Out in space beyond the earth's atmosphere are the primary cosmic rays. When these primary cosmic rays enter our atmosphere, they strike atoms and molecules of air, causing atomic explosions. From these explosions are formed many of the known particles of the atomic world. After collision, the weaker secondary cosmic rays stream on down to earth.

The Earth is bathed in these strange rays that reach us from the very depths of space. They come at the rate of about one per square centimeter per minute. Put another way, this means there are about 200 cosmic rays going through you and me every minute.

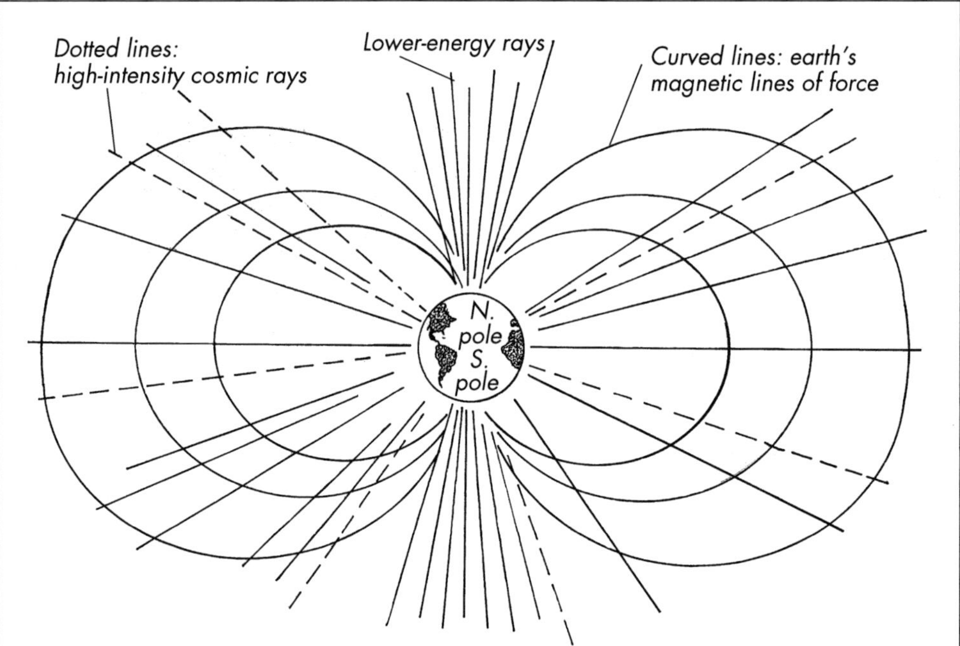

Figure 25-1. Cosmic rays are particles of high energy that reach earth from distant space. Lower-energy cosmic rays are bent by earth's magnetic field, and so arrive mainly at the magnetic poles. High-energy cosmic rays smash right through earth's magnetic lines of force (curved lines) and are distributed more or less evenly over earth. The dotted lines represent cosmic rays of high intensity. The continuous lines represent cosmic rays of low intensity.

Because cosmic rays are electrified particles, they are affected by the earth's magnetism. In fact, the magnetic field of the earth acts as a kind of magnetic sorter for cosmic rays. Low-energy cosmic rays are bent by the earth's magnetic lines of force and swept toward the north and south magnetic poles. High-energy cosmic rays smash right through the magnetic lines of force and appear at all latitudes (Figure 25-1). To study the high-energy rays, measurements are made at the equator. To study low-energy rays, measurements are made at the poles.

Sorting Out "Cosmic Rays"

You can make a magnetic sorter for "cosmic rays."

What you need: sheet of plastic, small boxes or blocks, strong bar magnet, 6 × 2-cm card folded into a "V" as in Figure 25-2, plasticene, ball bearings of various sizes

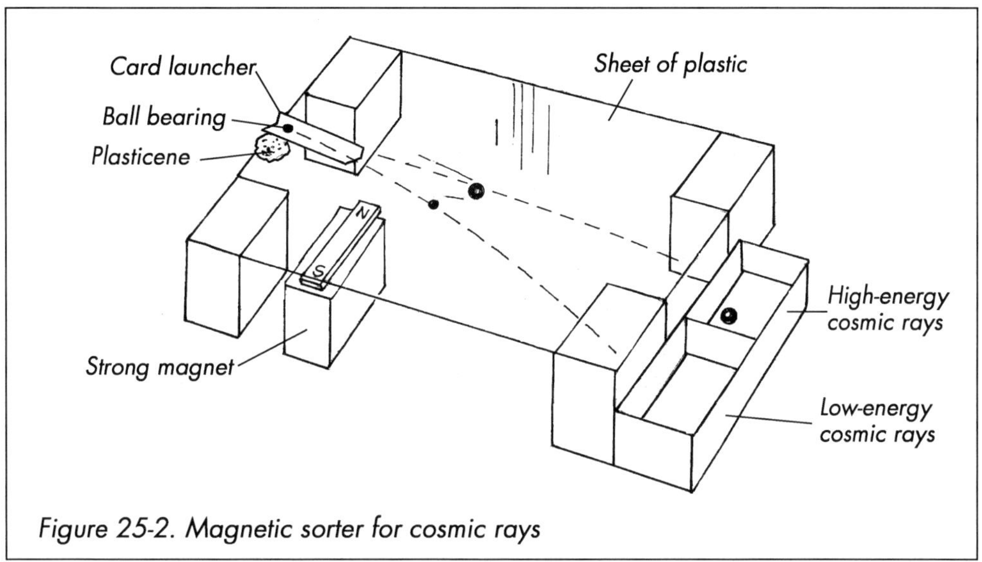

Figure 25-2. Magnetic sorter for cosmic rays

1. Arrange your magnetic sorter as shown in Figure 25-2. Try to have the strong bar magnet right next to the sheet of plastic. Support the "V" piece of card with a little plasticene to act as a launcher for the "cosmic rays," which are represented by the ball bearings.

2. Launch the larger and smaller ball bearings representing cosmic rays of different energies. What happens as they pass by the strong bar magnet? Do their courses bend or deflect in the magnetic field? You may need to experiment with the placing of the strong bar magnet to get the best results from your sorter.

3. Cosmic rays may come from a supernova. What is a supernova?

4. How does the earth's magnetic field act as a sorter for these mysterious rays that bombard our earth from space?

5. Make each sentence tell about cosmic rays by filling the space with one of the words under it:

   a. Cosmic rays are _____________________________ of very high energy.
      (sparks, particles, oxygen atoms)

   b. _____________________ cosmic rays are found outside our atmosphere.
      (Primary, Secondary)

   c. Cosmic rays travel at nearly the speed of _____________________________.
      (sound, light, a jet plane)

   d. Atoms in the air _____________________________ when cosmic rays strike them.
      (explode, spin quickly, vibrate)

e. Cosmic rays are _____________________ by earth's magnetic field. (not affected, deflected, weakened)

f. There are about _____________________ hundred cosmic rays passing through each of us all the time. (one, two, five)

26. Color Flame Tests

When a clean platinum wire is dipped into a salt (sodium chloride) solution, then placed in the flame of a Bunsen burner, the flame is brilliant yellow (as with sodium vapor streetlights). If the experiment is repeated with strontium chloride, the Bunsen flame takes on a bright red color. Lithium chloride gives a deep red, and calcium chloride, a brick red. Barium chloride is green, copper chloride is blue-green, and potassium chloride is lilac or violet.

In each experiment, the chemical substance gives off light of a specific color because its atoms are excited by an energy source—in this case, the flame of the Bunsen burner. When the excited atoms release this energy and return to their normal unexcited state, they emit light. It is this light that forms the distinctive color of the particular chemical.

Because metals burn with different colored flames, chemists test this way to identify chemicals. From their studies of the hot, glowing gases of a star billions of kilometers out in space, astronomers can tell which elements may be present there.

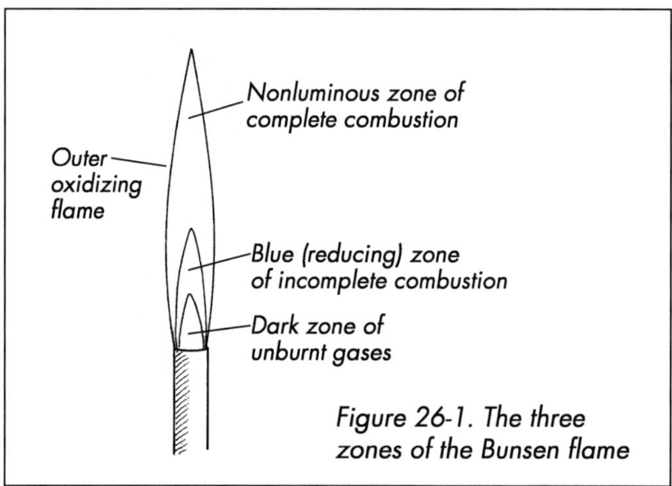

Figure 26-1. The three zones of the Bunsen flame

Color is the basis of the borax bead test. When borax is heated, it melts to form a glasslike substance in which metal oxides will dissolve. The compounds formed are sometimes highly colored, the color being a characteristic of the metal. So it is possible to say what metal is present in a chemical substance by the color it gives to the borax bead.

Making Colorful Flames

You can carry out some color flame tests and borax bead tests to identify elements. Be sure to attach your wire to some kind of handle that will not conduct too much heat to your hand.

What you need: wire (platinum—or use nichrome from an old heater element)*, Bunsen burner, boric acid, fine sandpaper, table salt, cream of tartar, lime (calcium oxide), copper sulphate (bluestone), borax, clean tin lid, alcohol, teaspoon, ferrous sulphate, concentrated hydrochloric acid

> **Warning:** Use extreme caution when using concentrated acids. Goggles, gloves, and aprons are *required* for this activity.

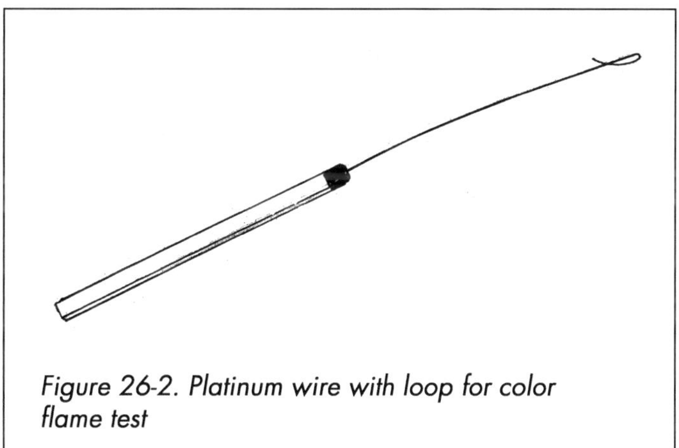

Figure 26-2. Platinum wire with loop for color flame test

1. Do a flame test on boric acid by putting $\frac{1}{4}$ teaspoon of the acid in a tin lid and cover with a teaspoon of alcohol (or methylated spirits). Set fire to the alcohol. Do you see a green flame—this is a test for boric acid which contains the element boron.

2. Make one end of the wire into a small loop. Now heat some table salt—sodium chloride—in the loop in the flame. Describe the color. This is a test for the element sodium. After each test, clean the wire loop with fine sandpaper.

3. Heat some cream of tartar in the loop. What color is the flame? Sprinkle some cream of tartar into the flame. What color do you see? This violet color is a test for potassium.

---

* Clean the platinum wire after each test by dipping in the concentrated acid, then heating; if nichrome wire is used, clean with fine sandpaper.

4. Try lime (calcium) and bluestone (copper). Describe the colors you see.

5. If you can get salts of strontium and barium, test these in the flame also. It is difficult to clean the wire after using these. Note the beautiful crimson that strontium salts give the flame. Strontium nitrate is used in making fireworks and for producing red flares.

6. You can also perform borax bead tests with the Bunsen flame. To make the bead, heat your wire to a red glow, then plunge it into the borax. The borax melts and sticks to the wire. Heat this again in the flame, plunge into the borax, and reheat. Continue doing this until you get a fine, clear bead of borax. To do the test, touch the hot bead to a little of the substance you are examining—e.g., copper sulphate. Heat in the burner, and note the color of the bead in the oxidizing and reducing parts of the flame. For example, with copper, the bead is pale blue (oxidizing flame), or red (reducing flame).
Chromium—The borax bead is green in both oxidizing and reducing flames.
Iron—The bead is dark green (reducing flame) or reddish-brown (oxidizing flame).
Cobalt—The bead is blue.
Nickel—In the oxidizing flame, nickel compounds color the borax bead brown.
Iron—The bead is red when hot and yellow when cold in the oxidizing flame, and green in the reducing flame.

7. Have a friend present you with some "unknowns." Carry out borax bead tests on these and decide which metal is present. Note: You must prepare a new bead for each new test. Simply hold the hot bead from the old test under running water and it will break up. Make sure the wire is perfectly clean before you proceed to the next test.

27. Magnetosphere and Solar Wind

They that go down to the sea in ships, that do business in great waters;
These see the works of the Lord, and his wonders in the deep.

—*Psalm 107*

Satellites have shown that the earth is surrounded by a magnetic field, or magnetosphere. Energetic particles from the sun are trapped in it. The two areas of the magnetosphere are known as the Van Allen radiation belts, after the American physicist James Van Allen. The belts take the form of two giant doughnuts that encircle the earth (Figures 27-1, 27-2). The first belt is about 3,000 kilometers (1,800 miles) out and reaches thousands of kilometers into space. Energetic particles (protons and electrons), plasma clouds, and other radiations spewed out by the sun determine the size and shape of the magnetosphere. This is especially true at the time of major solar flares, when the earth's magnetosphere and ionosphere are likely to be disturbed. Within the belts, the particles spiral backward and forward from pole to pole along the lines of magnetic force.

Beyond the Van Allen belts, fresh bursts of particles are constantly arriving in the solar wind. The solar wind is the steady stream of charged particles, protons and electrons, that the sun boils off. It blows through space at speeds of over 1,000,000 kilometers/hour (625,000 miles/hour). Out in space, the earth's magnetic field acts like a giant umbrella, deflecting the solar wind as it blows past. Where the solar wind first strikes the magnetic field, an immense shock wave is set up, like bow waves on a barge. The solar wind, so diverted by the magnetosphere, joins up again downstream some millions of kilometers from earth.

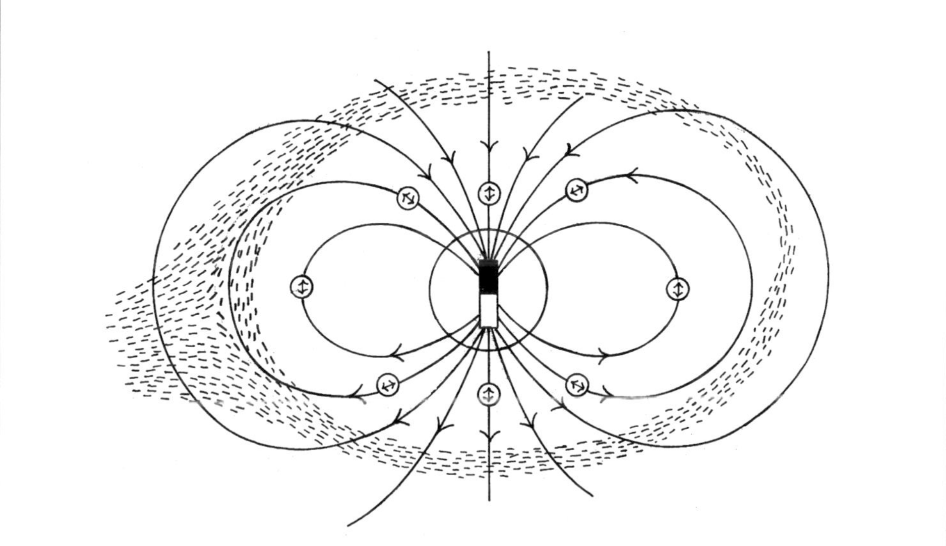

Figure 27-1. *The earth behaves as if it contains a great magnet, with its lines of force reaching far out into space many times earth's radius (6,500 km or 4,000 miles). The dotted lines represent particles from a solar explosion. The magnetic storms that follow on earth cause radio blackouts and interfere with long-distance communications.*

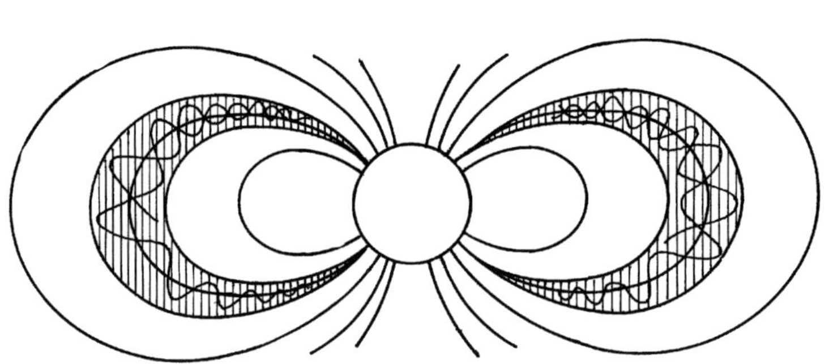

Figure 27-2. The Van Allen radiation belts. An important discovery made by satellites is the existence of high-energy particles circulating high above the ionosphere. There are two such belts, one inside the other, shaped rather like giant doughnuts and both having greatest breadth above the equator. The outer belt is 13,000 km (8,000 mi) above the earth and fatter on the sunward

At the tips of the Van Allen belts, charged particles trickle out into the high atmosphere of the earth. Here, they undergo collisions with the sparse atoms of the air they strike. When the excited atoms release the absorbed energy, the sky glows, giving the distinctive colors and patterns of the aurora—the weird lights in the skies about which a thousand tales are told.

Models of Earth's Magnetic Phenomena

You may make models of the magnetosphere, solar wind, and Van Allen belts, and demonstrate how they work.

What you need: bar magnet, card, iron filings, magnetic compass, magnetized knitting needle*, ball of wool yarn, plastic pot, insulated wire, 6-volt battery, switch, 7–8 pieces of magnetic strip** about 20 cm long each, cardboard box with top and bottom cut out, small globe or ball, tape, drinking straw, folded card

Model for Magnetosphere

1. Earth's magnetism is a mystery. Make a magnetic field by placing a bar magnet under a piece of card. Sprinkle iron filings on top. Sketch the "magnetosphere." Where are the particles most closely packed together? Where is the field strongest? What happens when you bring a compass into the field? Where is the earth's field strongest?

---

* Magnetize the needle by stroking 20 times in one direction only with a bar magnet.
**Obtain from a scientific warehouse or educational supply store.

2. Pass the magnetized knitting needle through the ball of wool and set the arrangement in the plastic pot. The ball represents the earth; the needle represents the magnetic field. Explore the "magnetosphere" with a compass (Figure 27-3). Where is it strongest? Where weakest? How far out beyond "earth" does the magnetic field act? Wherever you place the compass on "earth," how does it point? Take a pinch of iron filings between your fingers and allow them to trickle down onto your model. What happens to the iron particles? How is this like particles in the solar wind? How does the aurora come into the picture?

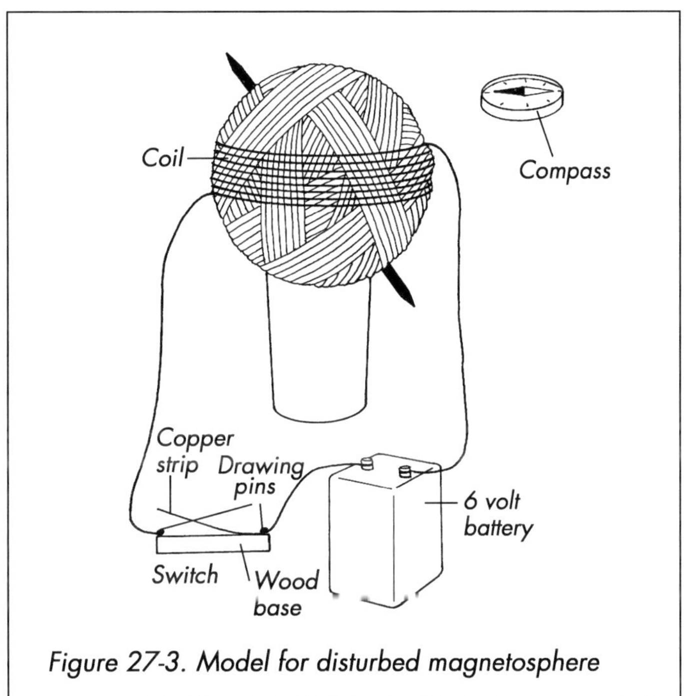

Figure 27-3. Model for disturbed magnetosphere

Model for Disturbed Magnetosphere

The magnetosphere often fluctuates during solar storms, such as sunspots and solar flares. To show how sudden shifts in the magnetosphere take place, wind a coil of 20 turns of plastic-coated hookup wire around the ball of wool. Connect it to the switch and battery as shown in Figure 27-3. Holding your compass near the "magnetosphere," close the switch. What happens? Is the compass needle affected? Does it shift or give another bearing? How do you relate this to geomagnetic storminess (magnetic storms on earth)? How is this related to disturbances in communication (in the ionosphere), the aurorae, and storms on the sun?

Model for Solar Wind

1. Use the setup as shown in Figure 27-4. The pieces of magnetic strip represent the earth's magnetic field reaching out into space beyond the globe. Place some iron

filings, representing charged particles from a gigantic solar explosion, on a piece of card. Puff through the straw. What happens? How is the magnetic field acting like a magnetic umbrella? What happens to the solar wind as it flows around the magnetic umbrella?

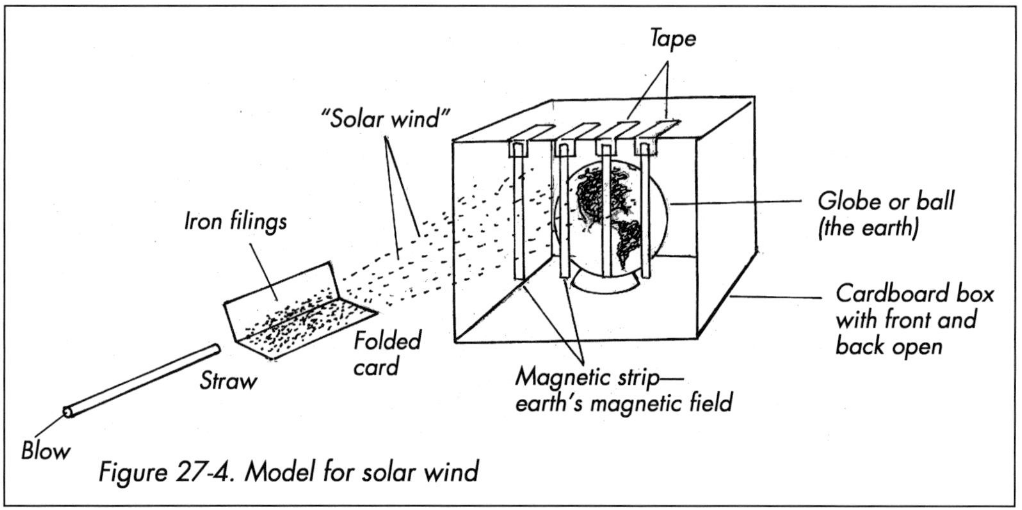

Figure 27-4. Model for solar wind

2. Find out how the magnetic umbrella is important to life on Earth. Write 3–4 sentences.

Model for Van Allen Belts

1. Use the same setup as in Figure 27-4 above, but this time, have another four pieces of magnetic strip hanging over the back of the box. Place the globe behind them. The front pieces of magnetic strip now represent the outer Van Allen belt, while those next to the globe are the inner.

2. Again, place some iron filings on a card. This time, puff more vigorously through the straw onto them. If the iron filings represent particles from a solar explosion, what happens to them? How is this like the Van Allen belts?

3. What kinds of atomic particles bombard the earth from space? Write a sentence telling about each of them.

4. Complete these sentences by writing the missing words in the spaces:

    a. The Van Allen r______________ belts consist of e______________ particles

    trapped by the earth's m____________ field.

b. The s__________ w____________ is made up of charged particles such as

p_____________ and e______________. When the solar wind reaches earth,

it is d______________ by the earth's m___________ field.

28. In the Beginning

> *In the beginning, God created the heavens and the earth.*
>
> —*Genesis 1:1*

Astronomers wish to know how the universe is built. They know that great swarms of stars are grouped together, forming "islands" of stars in space. The great English astronomer William Herschel called them "island universes." Today, we use the term "galaxy" for these great swarms of millions and millions of stars. In our own Milky Way galaxy there are some 200 billion stars. Large telescopes show billions of other galaxies fairly evenly distributed throughout space.

By studying the light from distant galaxies, scientists can tell how far away the galaxies are and how fast they are moving. The galaxies are moving away from us. The farther away the galaxy, the greater the speed of recession. If the galaxies are receding from us, there must have been a time in the past history of the universe when they were all much closer together. According to theory, all the universe's matter and energy was concentrated in a very small volume. This super-dense atom had enormous density, of the order of millions of tons per cubic centimeter.

Then, for some reason, the super-dense atom became unstable and blew apart in a catastrophic explosion. The results of that explosion we see in the sky today—in the formation of the galaxies as we know them, speeding away from each other. This is the "big bang" theory of how the universe started. The theory also holds that the universe is still expanding, carrying the galaxies along with it.

Modeling the Big Bang

You can make a model of the expanding universe using a balloon.

What you need: two large round balloons (white or light color), black felt-tip marker, tiny paper chips or rice puffs, pin, art materials

1. With the felt-tip pen, make dots about 2 cm apart over the surface of one of the balloons. Think of the balloon as the super-dense atom before the big bang took place.

2. Mark three of the dots 1, 2, and 3. Measure the distances from 1 to each of 2 and 3. Also measure the distance between 2 and 3.

3. Blow a little air into the balloon. The balloon represents the universe, which is expanding. The dots are the galaxies. Now measure the distances between galaxies 1, 2, and 3 again. What do you find? Suppose you lived on galaxy 2. Would the other galaxies seem to have moved away from you?

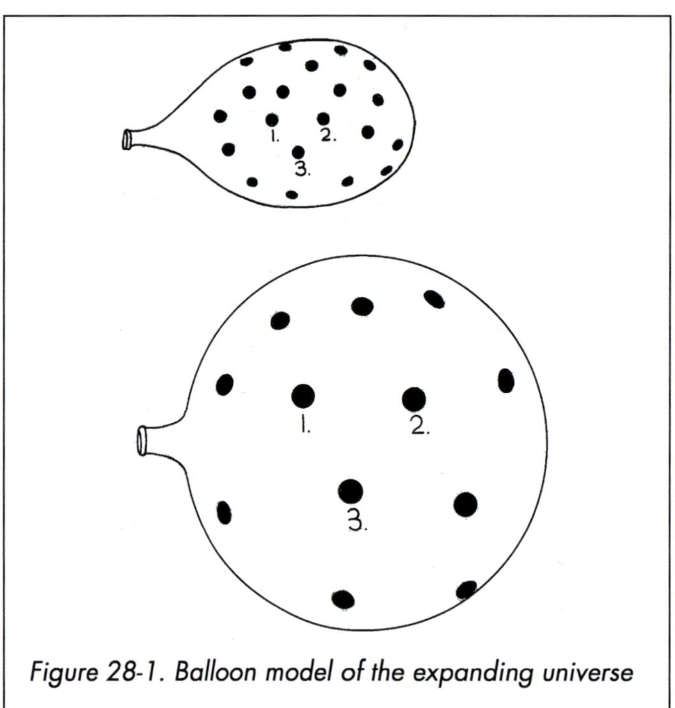

Figure 28-1. Balloon model of the expanding universe

4. Now fully inflate the balloon. Measure the distances between galaxies 1 and 2, 2 and 3, and 3 and 1. Describe what has happened.

5. You are an astronomer in galaxy 1. What do you see galaxies 2 and 3 doing? If you were on galaxy 2, what would you see galaxies 3 and 1 doing? What can you say about all the galaxies around you? How does this help give you a picture of a universe that is expanding—or blowing up before our eyes?

6. To simulate the big bang, the birth of the galaxies, and the idea of a runaway universe, deflate the balloon. Then pass 40–50 tiny chips of paper or puffed rice (or other light cereal) through the nozzle. Now inflate the balloon again fully, wave it around a bit to disperse the chips or cereal, then touch a pin to the balloon. The

bursting of the balloon is the big bang. The paper chips or cereal flying out in all directions show the violent birth and consequent expansion of the universe (Figure 28-2).

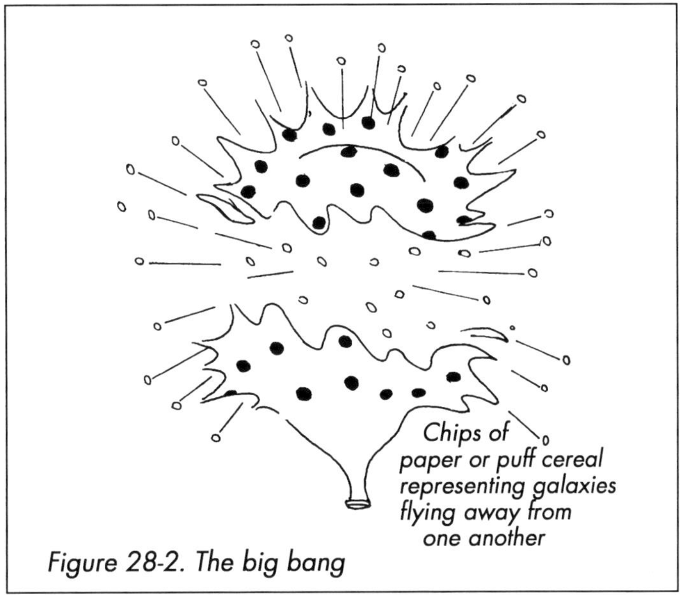

Figure 28-2. The big bang

7. Suppose the expansion of the universe slows down, gravity takes over, and the universe starts to contract until it reaches the big crunch—the big bang in reverse. Use the second balloon, which should be marked the same as the first. To show the big crunch, blow up the balloon, then allow it to gently deflate. You are turning the clock back; the universe is collapsing on itself. What do you notice about the galaxies (the dots)? What can you say about the density of the universe as collapse takes place? What about its volume? As the dots come closer together, you are approaching within milliseconds of the big bang—the primeval fireball that launched the universe on its career of expansion.

8. Write a paragraph on your experiments showing the big bang and the big crunch. Include some sketches of your demonstrations.

9. Study red shift and cosmic background radiation. Why are they evidence for the big bang?

10. Find out anything you can about the following scientists and an expanding universe: Vesto Melvin Slipher, the Abbé Georges Lemaître, Edwin Hubble.

11. Use art materials—wire, plasticene or modeling clay and so on—and a diagram from an astronomy book to make a mobile or model of the Local Group of Galaxies. Label your mobile appropriately and suspend it from the ceiling of your room. Find out what the letters M and NGC used on the diagram stand for.

29. Galaxies

In the view of astronomers today, the universe consists of billions of galaxies, each of which is made up of billions of stars. Our sun is one star in the Milky Way galaxy. Along with our sun are the planets and the constellations. Our galaxy is lens- or bicycle-wheel-shaped, and like other galaxies, it rotates. It takes 200 million years to complete one full turn. It is believed that 3 minutes after the big bang, hydrogen and helium nuclei formed, and after 300,000 years atoms formed from nuclei and electrons. But it was not for a billion years that protogalaxies condensed out of gas and dust. Our own galaxy would then have been born. In 10 billion years the sun and planets that make up our solar system formed in our Milky Way galaxy.

Galaxies are of three general types. A spiral galaxy has spiral arms reaching out from its center. Our own Milky Way galaxy is a spiral. Some galaxies are egg-shaped and are called ellipticals. Other galaxies have no special shape and are called irregulars (Figure 29-1).

About one billion galaxies can be seen with the world's largest telescopes, but only three can be seen with the naked eye. One of these is Andromeda; the other two are the Clouds of Magellan. Andromeda is about two million light years away. (A light year is the distance that light travels in one year.) When you look at this galaxy, the light entering your eye has been traveling through space for that time.

Photo 8. The Whirlpool Galaxy M51 is a spiral galaxy, as is our own Milky Way galaxy.

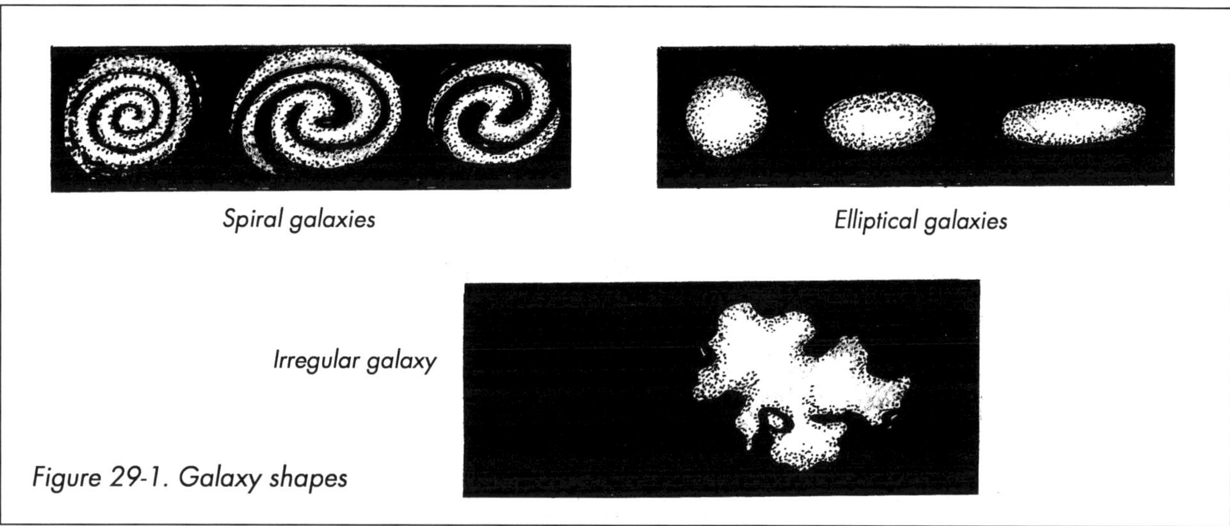

Figure 29-1. Galaxy shapes

Spinning Tea Leaves into Galaxies

You can show very nicely the shape of the galaxies.

What you need: three dessert plates or dishes (preferably white), water, used tea leaves, spoon

1. Put a teaspoon of used tea leaves in each of dessert plates A, B, and C, each plate being about three-quarters full of water. Give plate A a brisk circular stir with the spoon. Take out the spoon, and watch closely the patterns traced out by the tea leaves as they spiral in toward the center of the plate. Is the pattern rather like a rotating pinwheel? How does it compare with the picture shown on page 92, taken by one of the world's largest telescopes?

2. Repeat for plate B, but this time stir the water in an egg-shaped curve. Again watch the patterns of the moving tea leaves. Do they trace out ellipses or egg-shaped curves and give you the outline of an elliptical galaxy?

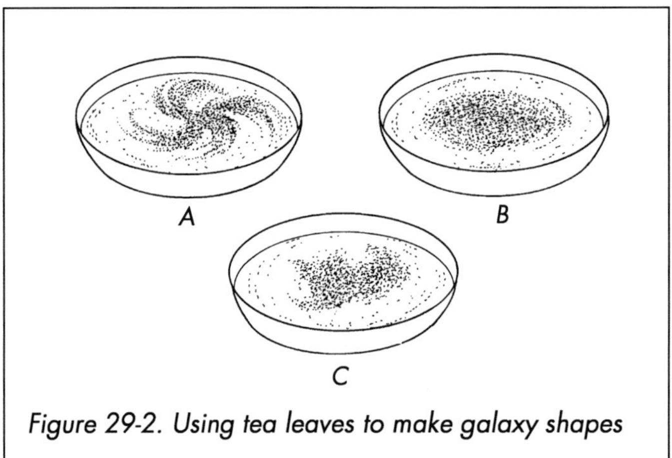

Figure 29-2. Using tea leaves to make galaxy shapes

3. Repeat for plate C, stirring the water this time in circles, then crisscross. Do the moving tea leaves trace out irregular patterns, with no particular form? Compare your results with the pictures in Figure 29-2.

4. What do you know about galaxies? Complete the paragraph below by writing the missing words in the spaces.

All the stars you can see in the sky belong to the M___________ W________

g__________. This galaxy is shaped like a l___________ or disc and is slowly

r_____________. It will take 200 years to complete a f__________ turn. Our galaxy

is a s_____________. Another type of galaxy is egg-shaped or e_____________. A

third type has no special s___________ and is called irregular.

30. How the Elements Were Formed

Atoms were once thought to be the smallest units of matter. However, now they are known to be made up of positive and negative charges called protons and electrons. A substance having an equal number of these particles is electrically neutral. Forces of electrical attraction between the charges keep the electrons revolving around the protons that form the center or nucleus of the atom. The Danish scientist Neils Bohr gave us a picture of the atom when he said, "An atom is like a miniature solar system, electron 'planets' whirling around a nucleus 'sun.'"

In 1932, Sir James Chadwick, an English physicist, discovered another particle, the neutron. Whereas the electron is only $\frac{1}{1840}$ the mass of the proton, the neutron's mass is nearly the same as the proton's, and it has no electric charge. These three particles—electron, proton, and neutron—are the building blocks for the 92 elements of nature. The atom of hydrogen, the simplest of all, has for its nucleus one proton or positive charge, with a single electron revolving around it. Hydrogen and another gas called helium make up 96–99 percent of the matter of the sun.

At the time of the big bang, the universe was extremely dense and hot with temperatures of trillions of degrees. Matter in its simplest form only—protons, neutrons, electrons, and neutrinos (particles without mass or charge)—were present. About 100 seconds after the big bang, the temperature had fallen to a billion degrees, and a proton striking a neutron would then form a nucleus of deuterium, an isotope of hydrogen. When two protons combined with a neutron, they formed an isotope of helium. Another neutron adding on could form ordinary helium.

When a few minutes had passed, the temperature of the universe had fallen to about 100 million degrees, too low for the nuclear reactions to continue. Formation of the elements in this way—called nucleosynthesis—then stopped, with helium making up 25–30 percent of the matter of the universe.

Only the lighter elements—hydrogen, deuterium, and helium, plus a trace of an isotope each of lithium and boron—would have been formed in the big bang. Nucleosynthesis of the heavier elements takes place in the interiors of stars like our sun, in supernovae explosions, and possibly in explosions in massive gas clouds throughout space. The heavier elements that make up our own bodies—the calcium and phosphorus that make up our teeth and bone and the iron of our red blood cells—have been formed in supernovae explosions and in stars within our own galaxy.

Building Atomic Models

You can make some atomic models.

What you need: 10 × 10-cm wood bases, wire, Ping-Pong balls (colored red for protons, black for neutrons), bonding adhesive, red and black felt-tip pens, plasticene or modeling clay, cardboard squares (about 5 × 5 cm), red and black jujubes (use red for protons and black for neutrons), toothpicks, pins, hatpins, workshop tools

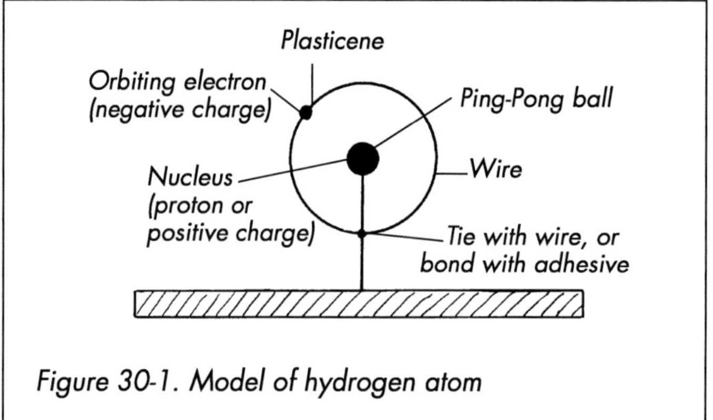

Figure 30-1. Model of hydrogen atom

1. Make the Ping-Pong ball models for the atoms of hydrogen and helium as shown (Figures 30-1 and 30-2). Note as you make them that the mass of an atom is in the nucleus. It is made up of protons or positive charges, each having unit mass, and neutrons with no electric charge and with mass nearly the same as a proton. Around the nucleus whirl electrons or negative electric charges. Each of the 92 elements in nature is given an atomic number. This tells you the number of protons in the nucleus. It is the same as the number of electrons in the electrically neutral atom. What makes up the nucleus of the hydrogen atom? What is its atomic number? What does this tell you? What makes up the nucleus of the helium atom? What is the atomic number? How many orbiting electrons are there? What can you say about electric charges in the atoms of hydrogen and helium you have made?

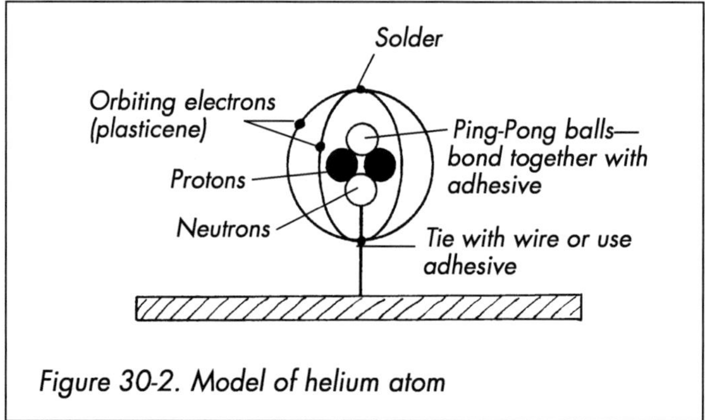

Figure 30-2. Model of helium atom

2. Make models for hydrogen, deuterium, and tritium (another hydrogen isotope), using jujubes, pins, hatpins, cardboard, and plasticene (Figure 30-3). Deuterium and tritium are described as isotopes of hydrogen. Write a sentence or two explaining what this means. What is the atomic number for each of these: hydrogen, deuterium, and tritium? What are the mass numbers? H_2O is the formula for drinking water. Find the formula for heavy water. How is heavy water important?

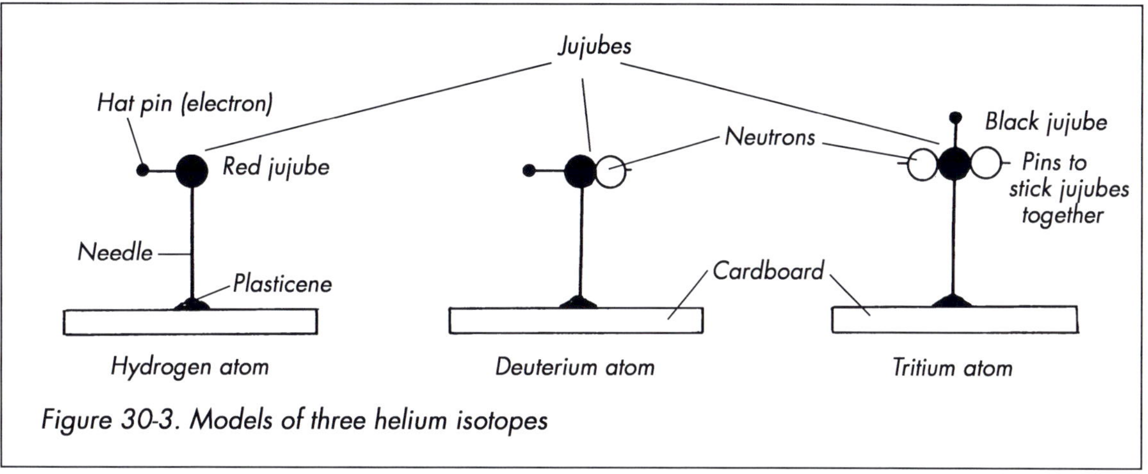

Figure 30-3. Models of three helium isotopes

3. Use your models to show how elements were formed in the big bang:

   a. a proton striking a neutron

   b. two protons combining with a neutron

4. In Figure 30-4, the "plus" balls are protons, the black ones neutrons. Count the protons only, then look at the chart and write the name of the element to which this nucleus belongs.

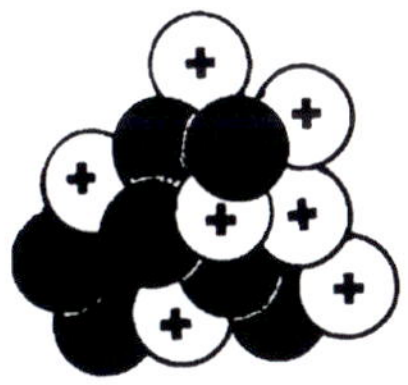

Figure 30-4. This represents a nucleus of which element?

Typical Atoms					
Element	**Protons** (also Atomic Number)		**Neutrons**		**Atomic Mass**
Nitrogen	7	+	7	=	14
Oxygen	8	+	8	=	16
Iron	26	+	30	=	56
Gold	79	+	118	=	197
Lead	82	+	125	=	207
Uranium	92	+	146	=	238

5. Write a paragraph telling how hydrogen and helium were important in the early stages of the universe.

31. Images from Space

> *Far away, hidden from the eyes of daylight,*
> *there are watchers in the skies.*
>
> —Euripides, ca. 406 B.C.

Images from flyby spacecraft may enable us to recognize life on other planets. Until quite recently this had never been attempted. But the *Galileo* spacecraft, on a mission to Jupiter, was able to make close-up examinations of planet Earth. While *Galileo's* instruments were not designed for an earth-encounter mission, they gave an opportunity for a control experiment—the search for life on planet Earth using a typical planetary probe. *Galileo* images showed four things that indicated life on Earth:

- An abundance of molecular oxygen (O_2) in the earth's atmosphere.
- Evidence of chlorophyll, the green pigment present in all plants.
- A trace amount of the gas methane (CH_4). Methane (or marsh gas, as it is known) rapidly oxidizes to H_2O and CO_2. Not a single molecule of methane would remain on Earth unless life processes replenished the methane supply.
- Finally, radio wave emissions indicated the existence of an advanced technological civilization on earth.

Searching for Life's Requirements on Earth

You can investigate some of the requirements for life on planet Earth.

What you need: candle, soup plate, water, jar or bottle, limewater, drinking straw, bicycle pump, salt, aquarium (if available), oxygen weed (Elodea or Spirogyra), funnel, test tube, hydrogen peroxide, manganese dioxide (or the black powder from an old battery), wood splint, two large beakers, barley grains

1. Burning and breathing use up oxygen: Is all the air we take in used up in breathing? To find out, light the candle and let a few drops of liquid wax drop onto the center of the plate. Press the unlit end of the candle onto this so that it stands upright. Now half fill the soup plate with water, light the candle, and carefully lower the jar or bottle upside down over it (Figure 31-1). What happens to the water level when the flame goes out? You could measure the depth of "air" in the jar before and after the level alters to find out approximately how much air has been used up in the burning. This is oxygen. What would happen if an animal were kept in the bottle?

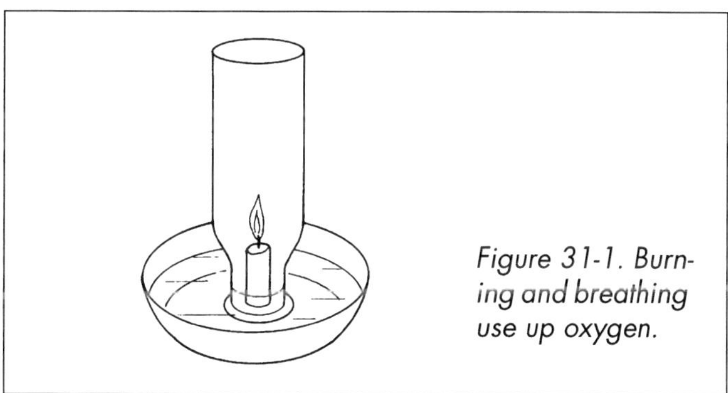

Figure 31-1. Burning and breathing use up oxygen.

2. Breathing gives off carbon dioxide: Is the air we breathe out different from ordinary air? Breathing, which gives us life, means taking in air and giving out carbon dioxide. Carbon dioxide turns limewater milky. Find out whether you breathe out carbon dioxide by blowing into limewater with a straw (Figure 31-2). What happens? Explain. Then repeat, using a bicycle pump.

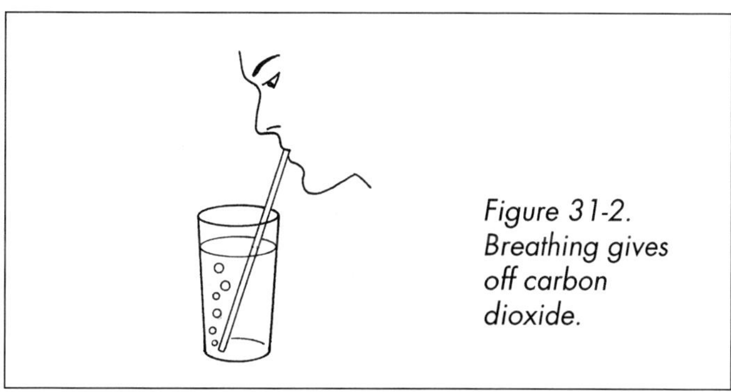

Figure 31-2. Breathing gives off carbon dioxide.

3. Air in water: Does water contain air? Run water from a tap into a jar or bottle and allow it to stand. What do you think the tiny bubbles are (Figure 31-3)? Where do they come from? When the air bubbles have stopped rising, pour a teaspoon of salt into the bottle and shake it. Does this bring more bubbles out of the water? Warm some water in the sun. Does this drive air out of water? Why should an aquarium be kept in a cool place? How is air in water important to life in water?

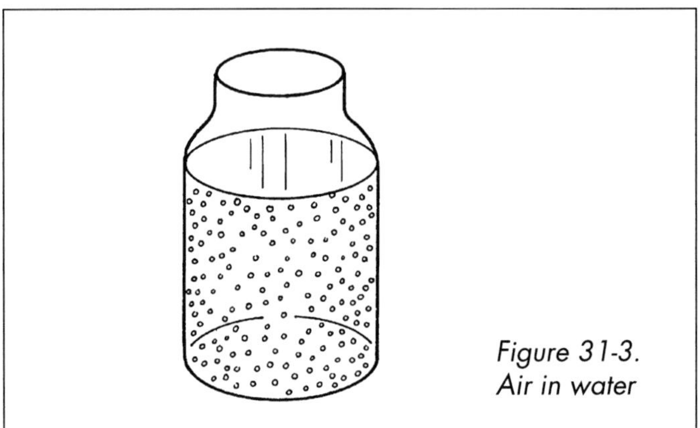

Figure 31-3.
Air in water

4. Plants make oxygen: Why do we have plants in an aquarium? Find out by placing a jar of water and oxygen weed in the sun to drive off bubbles of oxygen. Or, set up an experiment with a funnel and test tube to collect oxygen (Figure 31-4). If you wish to make oxygen, put 2–3 cm of hydrogen peroxide in a test tube and add a little manganese dioxide (you can use the black powder from an old battery). What happens? Does the mixture fizz up? Can you make the gas in the test tube rekindle a glowing wood splint? How is oxygen needed for burning in living things?

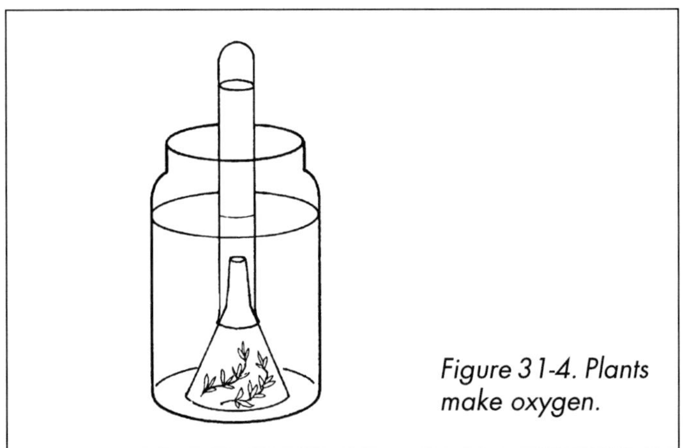

Figure 31-4. Plants
make oxygen.

5. Effect of oxygen: In each of two large beakers in a sink, place 10 soaked barley grains. Then cover each with a wide-mouth funnel as in Figure 31-5. Now fill each beaker with water that has been boiled and allowed to cool. Allow a very gentle stream of water from the tap to pass down one funnel, giving these seeds a supply of

water that contains air. Leave the setup alone for 6–7 days. What do you find when you look at the barley grains again? Which seeds have germinated better than the others? Explain why.

6. Have a discussion about the needs of living things. Animals need oxygen for breathing. They breathe out carbon dioxide into water or the atmosphere. Plants need carbon dioxide for food-making, but they give out oxygen into the atmosphere or water for the animals. Plants and animals balance each other perfectly. Oxygen comes from the air and carbon dioxide escapes into the air. How important is this in the ecology of planet Earth?

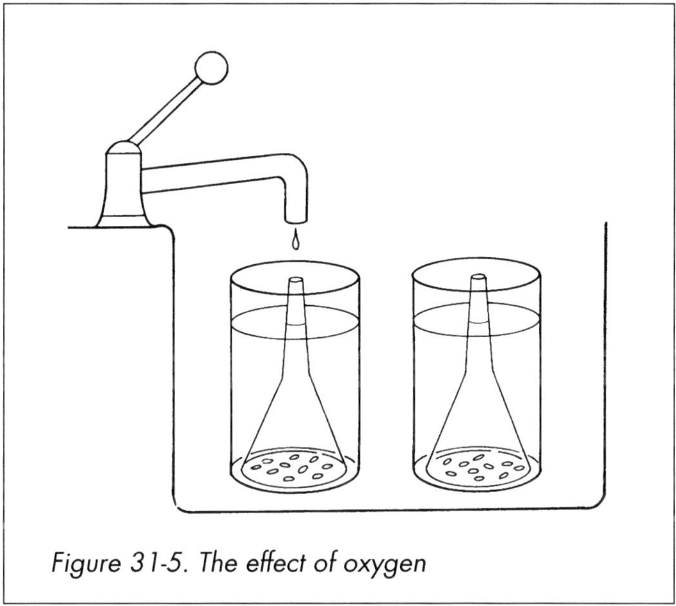

Figure 31-5. The effect of oxygen

Plant:	$6CO_2 + 6H_2O$	Sunlight $\longrightarrow$ Chlorophyll	$C_6H_{12}O_6 + 6O_2 \uparrow$
Animal:	$C_6H_{12}O_6 + 6O_2$	$\longrightarrow$	$6CO_2 \uparrow + 6H_2O +$ Energy

Plants and animals balance each other perfectly.

32. *Galileo* Mission to Jupiter

The *Galileo* spacecraft was launched from the space shuttle *Atlantis* on October 18, 1989. *Galileo* engineers designed a new interplanetary flight path using several gravity-assist swing-bys. *Galileo* went once around Venus and twice around Earth, shooting rather like a slingshot at the giant planet Jupiter. The flight path is known as the Venus-Earth-Earth-Gravity-Assist, or VEEGA, trajectory.

Photo 9. The Galileo *spacecraft and its inertial upper stage (IUS) are about to be released from the space shuttle* Atlantis *while in orbit, to begin a six-year journey to Jupiter. On the left is the earth's horizon, with a thin line representing its airglow and atmosphere.*

In addition to Earth and Venus flybys, *Galileo* became the first spacecraft to fly by two asteroids—Gaspra and Ida. In the flyby, two of *Galileo's* instruments detected a small moon, later named Dactyl, in orbit around Ida. *Galileo's* instruments also made direct observations of the impact of comet Shoemaker-Levy fragments with Jupiter in July 1994.

Communications with *Galileo* are via NASA's Deep Space Network; tracking stations are used in California, in Spain, and at Tidbinbilla, near Canberra, Australia. Unfortunately, *Galileo's* large main umbrella-like antenna failed to unfurl, and mission controllers have had to rely on a smaller, less capable antenna.

On July 13, 1995, *Galileo* released its atmospheric entry probe for its solo flight to Jupiter. On December 8, the probe descended into Jupiter's atmosphere, entering at the planet's equator and traveling in the same direction as the planet's rotation. During entry, the probe was surrounded by incandescent gases and subjected to tremendous forces as it decelerated from 170,000 km/hr to 160 km/hr in just two minutes.

The new data gathered may force scientists to rethink their theories about how Jupiter and the rest of the solar system formed. During its 57-minute descent into Jupiter's atmosphere, the probe detected fewer clouds than scientists expected, less helium, carbon, and oxygen than thought, 300° C temperatures, and stronger winds. The winds arise primarily because of a deep upwelling of heat from centers within the planet. Unlike Earth, Jupiter's heat is produced not by the sun, but by the planet itself.

Photo 10. Heat inside of Jupiter causes the planet's strong surface winds.

The probe traveled 600 kilometers (373 miles) into Jupiter's atmosphere before it burned up, through such gases as ammonia and hydrogen sulphide (a gas also formed by rotten eggs). The probe revealed that Jupiter is also drier than scientists thought. Because of the lack of water, lightning strikes the planet only about one tenth as often as on Earth. Scientists expected to find more water. They now have to decide if the planets in the solar system were formed from gases that gravitated into solid masses, or from masses bombarded by comets and asteroids.

Studying the Nature of Jupiter

You can show upwelling of gases due to heat, heating by friction, and gases detected by the Jupiter probe. And you can make a model of the Jovian atmosphere.

What you need: glass or metal tube, oily rag, candle, matches, piece of wood, wood saw, hand drill, ammonium chloride, sodium carbonate, test tubes, red litmus paper, sodium thiosulphate, vinegar, heater or burner, hair shampoo of the thick creamy (pearlescent) variety, food coloring, fishbowl or flask, turntable

1. Upwelling of gases due to heat: Heat a piece of metal or glass tubing as shown (Figure 32-1). Have the lower end over a piece of smoldering oily rag. (CAUTION! Place in water after use. The glass is HOT!) What do you notice about the movement of air gases due to heat, as shown by the smoke? How is this like what the probe detected in Jupiter's atmosphere? Research what might be causing the heating effect on Jupiter.

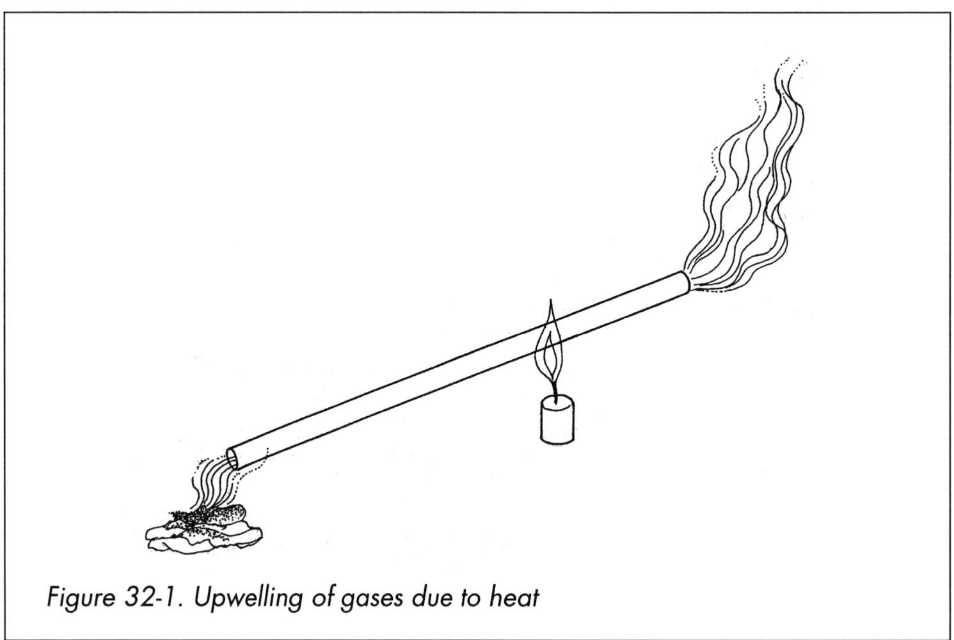

Figure 32-1. Upwelling of gases due to heat

2. Frictional heating: Press a finger hard on your coat and rub it back and forth quickly. What do you note? Saw and drill the piece of wood. How warm do the metal saw and drill get? Strike a match. How does friction help? In each of the above, explain, in terms of particle theory, how heat is produced. How did frictional heating cause the Jupiter probe to burn up?

3. Gases in Jupiter's atmosphere:

    a. Ammonia. Put $\frac{1}{2}$ teaspoon of sodium carbonate in a test tube and dissolve in 2–3 cm of water. Add $\frac{1}{2}$ teaspoon of ammonium chloride and heat. Wave your hand over the top of the test tube toward you. Do you detect the smell of ammonia? Hold a piece of moist red litmus paper at the mouth of the test tube and note what happens. Can you explain why?

    > WARNING: Use the following technique for testing odors:
    >
    > 1. Wear goggles and gloves.
    >
    > 2. Hold the test tube away from you.
    >
    > 3. Use your free hand to waft the gaseous substance toward you.

    b. Hydrogen sulphide. Put a few crystals of sodium thiosulphate in a dry test tube and heat. Describe what happens. Heat more strongly and note what forms in the upper, cooler part of the test tube. What smell do you notice? To the cool test tube, add a little vinegar (acid). What do you now notice about the smell of hydrogen sulphide? Why? What other gases make up Jupiter's atmosphere?

4. Model for Jupiter's atmosphere: Jupiter's equator rotates faster than the rest of the planet. For a planet 1,300 times bigger than earth, this sets up terrific storms and turbulence in the seething atmosphere. To make your model, mix the hair shampoo with water to make a thickish solution, then add the food coloring to simulate the color of Jupiter's atmosphere. Pour this into a good-sized flask or fishbowl and support it on a turntable (Figure 32-2). To see what storms and turbulences in Jupiter's atmosphere may look like, set the turntable spinning with your hands. Describe any patterns of turbulence or storminess you see in the spinning bowl. As the bowl slows down, how do the patterns change? How are differences in fluid friction playing a part? Spin the bowl again, then stop it with your hands. What do you see? Spin the bowl again, then stop it and spin it in the opposite direction. Describe any turbulence or storminess. How do your observations compare with information in your library books about Jupiter?

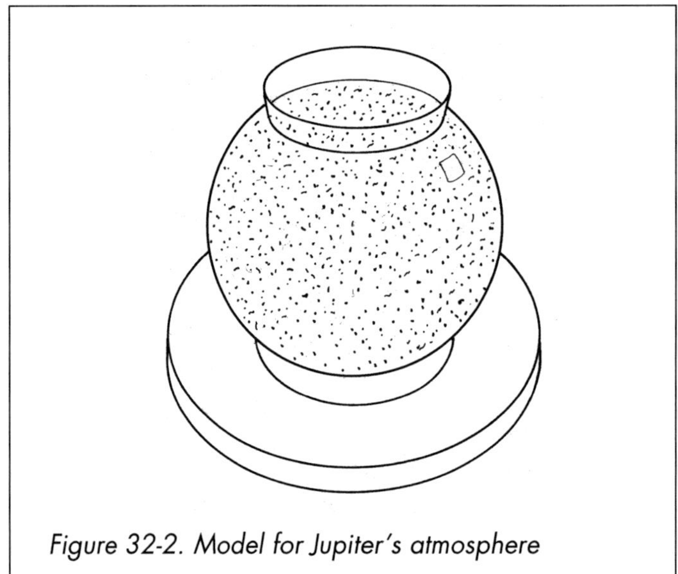

Figure 32-2. Model for Jupiter's atmosphere

33. The Hubble Orbiting Telescope

> *A good mirror is to the astronomer, a thing of beauty and a joy forever.*
>
> —Rev. W.E.A. Ellison

The Hubble Space Telescope (HST) acts very much like a ground observatory. In principle, it is the same as the reflecting telescopes invented by Guillaume Cassegrain and James Gregory in the seventeenth century.

Launch weight was about 11,000 kilograms (25,500 lb). Its length is 13.1 m (43.5 ft), and its diameter, 4.27 m (14 ft). Two large solar panels that unfold in space measure 2.3 by 11.8 m (7.8 by 39.4 ft) in orbit. Images from the telescope are radioed to earth by Tracking and Data Relay Satellites in geosynchronous orbit over the Atlantic and Pacific oceans.

The space telescope includes an optical telescope, a support systems module, and scientific instruments. They all work together as one unit in space to return images and other information to earth.

The Cassegrain telescope is the heart of the spacecraft. In this type of telescope, light from a star or other object travels through the aperture, down the assembly past the smaller secondary mirror, and strikes the large 2.4-m (94.5-in) primary mirror. The light then reflects back 4.6 m (16 ft) to the 0.3-m (12.2-in) secondary mirror, where it is concentrated into a small diameter beam. The beam travels through the 60-cm (24-in) hole in the primary mirror to the focal plane, 1.5 m (4.9 ft) behind its front surface.

Pictures and other scientific data are converted to electronic signals and transmitted via high-gain antennas at a rate up to one megabit (one million bits) per second. After being received on earth, the data is converted into images and spectrograms.

Photo 11. The Hubble Space Telescope took this image of the galaxy M100 on December 31, 1993. Hubble can identify rare pulsating stars, called Cepheid Variable stars, that are embedded in M100's spiral arms. Their pulsating light helps astronomers judge cosmic distances. In the image, the areas that appear blue contain hot, newborn stars.

Five scientific instruments are located behind the primary mirror, at the focal plane, where they can pick up the light from the telescope. These are the wide field/planetary camera, faint object spectrograph, high-resolution spectrograph, high-speed photometer, and the faint object camera. In addition there are fine guidance sensors, which because of their ability to accurately locate stars, are considered a sixth instrument. All these instruments are exchangeable during maintenance visits by astronauts during orbit.

The simple parabolic* mirror in the HST acts as a very useful light collector for the spacecraft, yielding more data in a short time than that gained over decades on earth.

---

* A hollowed-out or concave mirror shaped rather like the inside of a car headlight. It collects and focuses incoming light.

The space telescope is peering far out into the cosmos, giving the clearest images of galaxies, star systems, quasars, and exploding stars. It is also searching for extra-solar planets. The HST is able to do this by seeing the universe 600 kilometers above the masking influence of the atmosphere, gathering its information in its great 2.4-meter mirror. The distortion that occurs with earth-based instruments is not present. The HST space telescope sees objects 50 times dimmer than any seen before and it observes for 40 percent of a 24-hour day, on average.

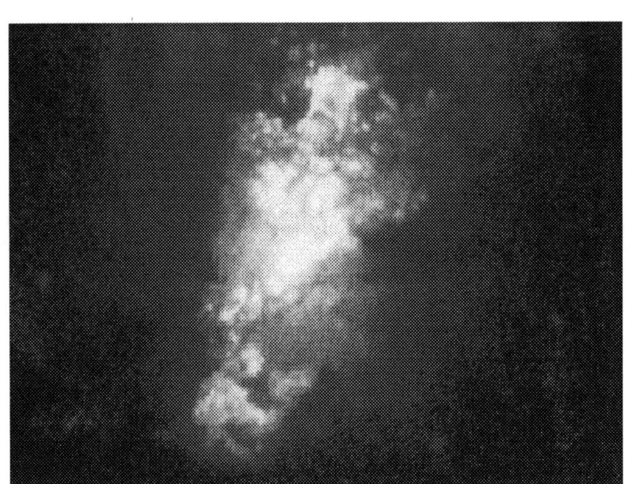

Photo 12. Hubble took this image of the nuclear region of the galaxy NGC 1068. With Hubble's observations, it will now be possible to compare images taken at various wavelengths of light to help us understand the mysterious source of the galaxy's intense energy— perhaps a hidden black hole.

Exploring How a Space Telescope Works

You can investigate how the Hubble Telescope is kept stable in orbit and does not topple or nosedive. You can also find out how curved mirrors work.

What you need: bicycle wheel, cord, 30-cm rod, washers, top, string, sheet of white paper, concave (curved-in) mirror, bottle (with cork or cap), half-filled with clear water, tablespoon (shiny), piece of white card with slots cut in it as shown, waxed paper

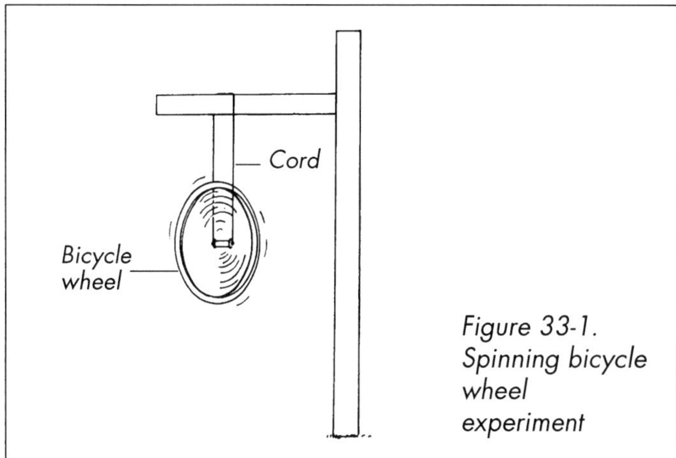

Figure 33-1.
Spinning bicycle
wheel
experiment

1. Try the experiment with the bicycle wheel as shown in Figure 33-1. To do this, support both sides of the axle with cords, then set the wheel spinning as fast as you can. Now slip one cord away from the axle. What happens? Does the wheel fall away? Why does the wheel keep spinning—slowly turn around? How is the wheel acting like a gyroscope? Now replace the axle with a smooth-fitting rod about 30 cm (12 in) long. Fit large washers on either side. Hold the ends of the rod with the wheel in front of you and have a friend spin the wheel rapidly. Try to tilt the wheel. Can you? Walk straight ahead with the wheel spinning fast, then try to turn at a 90° angle. Can you? What do you note as soon as you try to turn or tilt the wheel? What difference do you note with a larger, heavier wheel? How does spin help with stability? How are stability problems solved in the HST?

2. Spin the top. Does it seem to defy the law of gravity? How does spin help the top to achieve stability (Figure 33-2)? How does the energy of motion help to keep you upright on a bicycle? How does it help to balance birds and planes? Research how gyroscopes are used to point and track the Hubble Telescope. See also Activity 10, Inertia Wheels (page 33).

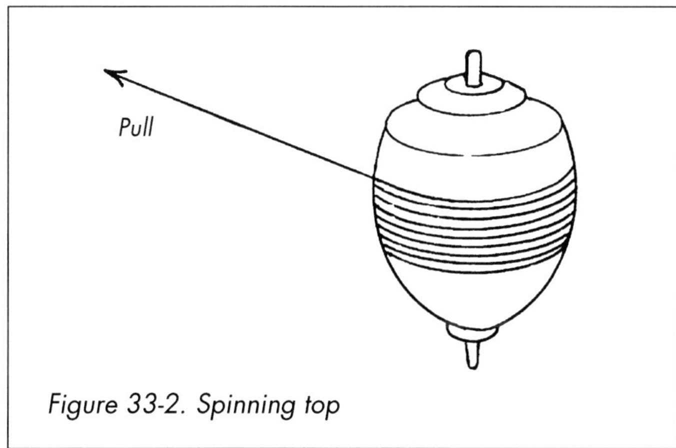

Figure 33-2. Spinning top

3. Find a window facing away from the sun. Tape white paper to the nearby wall to act as a screen. Do this on a bright, sunny day. Hold the concave mirror facing the window and move it to and from the paper and window (Figure 33-3). At a certain distance, what do you see on the paper? How would you describe the image—right side up or upside down? In color or black and white? How is this like Hubble's mirror?

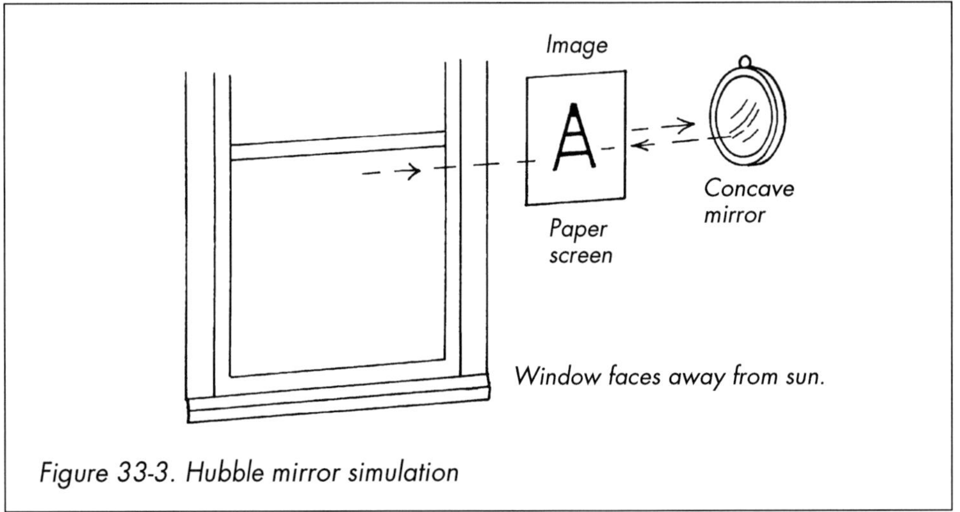

Figure 33-3. Hubble mirror simulation

4. With your face close to the concave mirror, look into it. How would you describe the image? Now move back slowly. What happens to the image? Now move back a little further. How does the image change? Now where you stand, hold upside down a bottle half-filled with water (Figure 33-4). Describe how you see the bottle. Can you explain why?

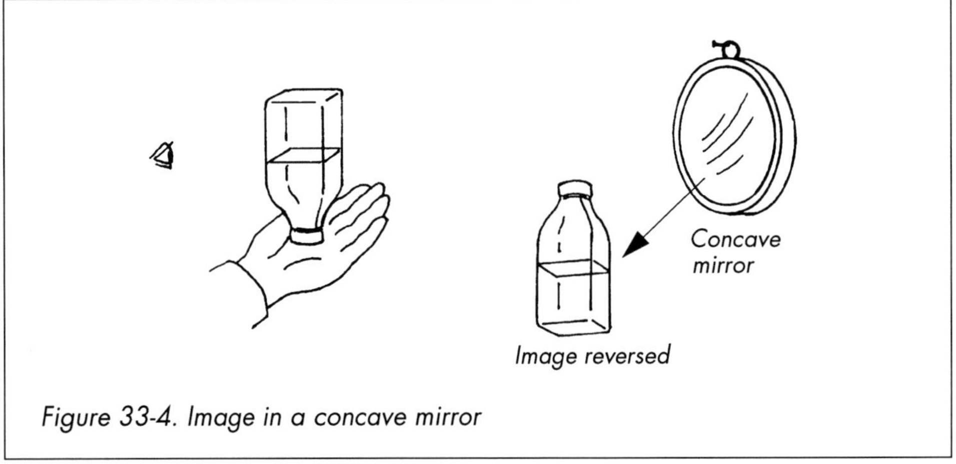

Figure 33-4. Image in a concave mirror

5. Hold the piece of slotted cardboard in sunlight as shown in Figure 33-5 and reflect the sun's rays from the concave (in-curving) side of the tablespoon. What do you see the reflected sun's rays do? How is this like Hubble's mirror?

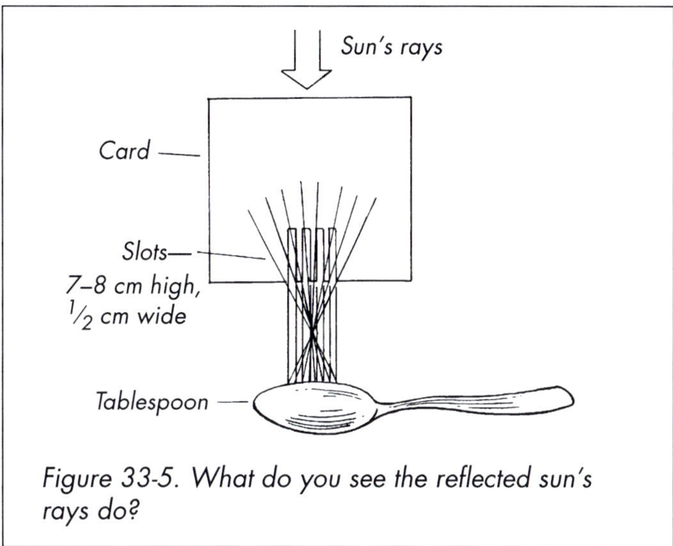

Figure 33-5. What do you see the reflected sun's rays do?

6. On the piece of waxed paper, place four teaspoons of iron filings as in Figure 33-6. Using each in turn you can make galaxy models.

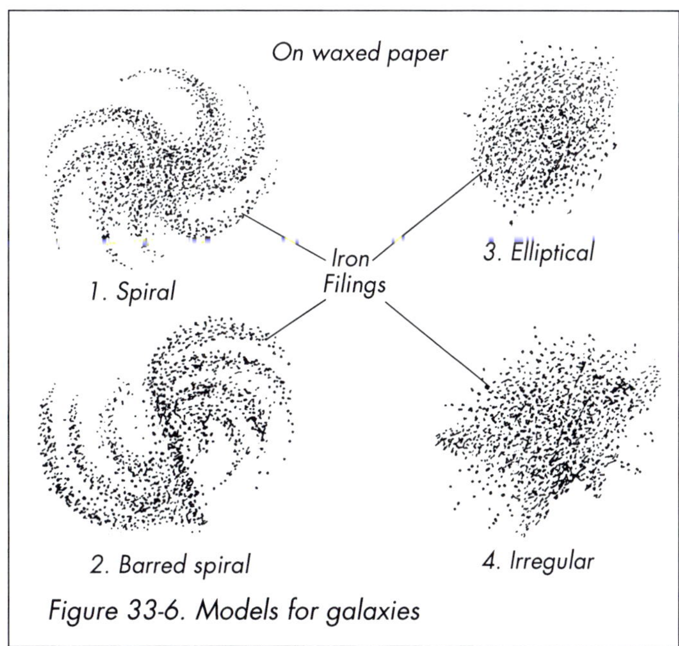

Figure 33-6. Models for galaxies

Galaxies by Finger-Forming Figures A, B, C, D, 1 to 4.

a. Spiral Galaxy. Pile 1. Use a finger and little filings to form the nucleus of the galaxy; then make spiral arms winding out from it. Some little bits and grains of filings here and there can represent gas and dust within the galaxy.

b. Barred Spiral Galaxy. Pile 2. As above; form a nucleus with a bar running through it. Then form spiral arms which loop away from the ends of the bar.

c. Elliptical Galaxy. Pile 3. Make the filings into two rounded or egg-shaped forms. Have one small and one large, for elliptical galaxies vary greatly in size, from giants to dwarfs.

d. Irregular Galaxy. Pile 4. Form your filings into an odd or irregular shape, neither spiral nor elliptical. Have some filings and grains around for gas and dust. Now carefully place your piece of waxed paper on a hot plate for a few seconds. Then remove. The effect of the heat is to soften/melt the wax, trapping the iron filings, so making your galaxies permanent. Use a felt-tip pen to label your galaxies and set up a classroom display.

34. Are We Alone in the Universe?

How we began, where and when we began, and whether we are alone in the universe are mysteries we have puzzled over for centuries. The Greeks had taught that planet Earth was not the sole dwelling place for living beings. Lucretius, the Roman writer, wrote in the first century B.C., "... in other regions of space there exist other earths inhabited by other peoples and animals."

Our home in space is a small planet in a solar system moving around an average-sized star, one of 200 billion similar stars of the Milky Way galaxy. Our sun and its planets are neatly tucked away in one of the outer suburbs of just one of the many galaxies that make up our universe. Some estimate there are a billion stars with planets capable of supporting life in our own galaxy. Many people believe there are dozens of communicating civilizations within 50–100 light years of our earth.

Our galaxy, then, may be teeming with life. As many as one star in ten may have planets around it. Such a star and planet would seem to move from side to side as they orbited around the center of gravity. The planet, of small mass, would have a large orbit, while the star, of large mass, would have a small orbit. A special long-focal-length telescope searches for these tiny wobbles. We cannot see planets directly, but we can see the secondary effect of wobble.

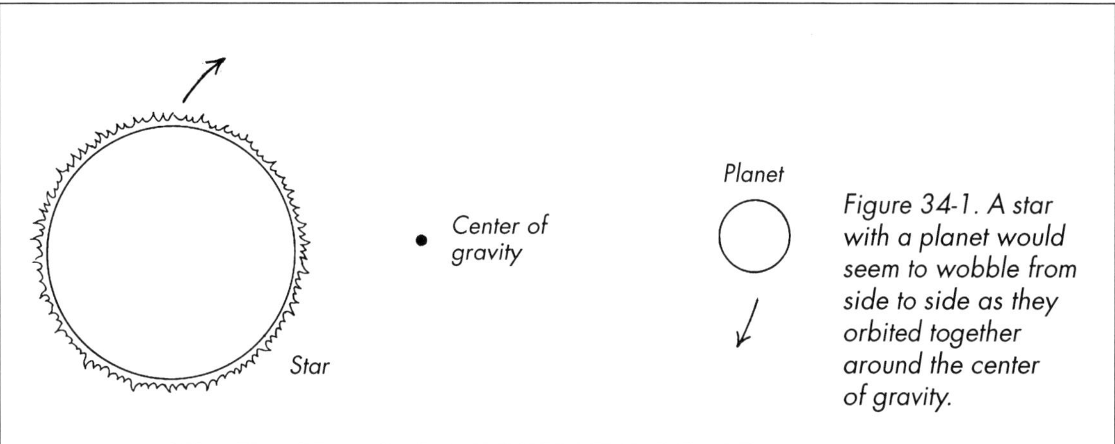

Figure 34-1. A star with a planet would seem to wobble from side to side as they orbited together around the center of gravity.

By taking many photographs, astronomers can detect movements of stars, but the method is slow. Using a new electronic device with a photon counter, as much information is obtained in one hour as in one year by the older method. Using the new method, astronomers will be able to see planets down to the size of those in our solar system around 500 of the nearest stars. The Hubble Space Telescope is also contributing to the search.

Detecting Planetary Orbits and Life

You can show how astronomers would detect another star with planets going around it like our sun. You can also look at one way a spacecraft would search for life on another planet.

What you need: thin strip of wood about 50 cm long, a pivot for this (e.g., a nail in a block of wood as support), large ball for the sun, small ball for the earth (use plasticene or modeling clay), three saucers with glass or plastic covers OR use petri dishes, two 20-cm pieces of string, gelatin, boiling water

1. Place the small and large plasticene balls at the ends of the wood strip. Balance the strip on your finger to find the center of gravity. Then with a bradawl (a chisel-like awl), make a small dimple in the strip. Balance the arrangement on the nail and have a friend spin the sun/planet system, while you watch it from the other side of the room (Figure 34-2). Describe the orbit the sun and planet seem to have. From your viewpoint, do the sun and planet seem to wobble from side to side? If scientists detect tiny wobbles in the movement of a star, what might they conclude?

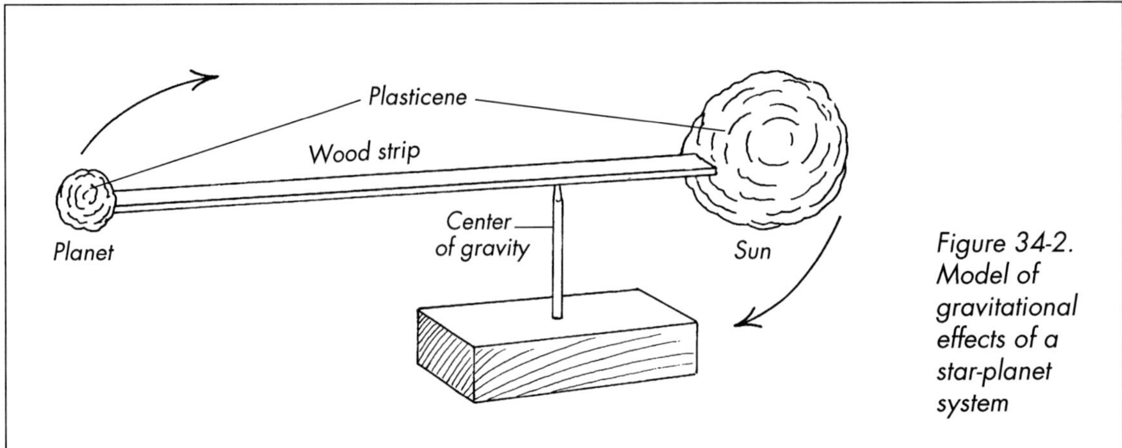

Figure 34-2. Model of gravitational effects of a star-planet system

2. Place the three saucers in boiling water for about 10 minutes to sterilize them. Then remove them with tongs. Into each, pour liquid gelatin about $\frac{1}{2}$ cm deep. Cover each with a glass or plastic square (OR use the petri dishes here). Drag one string over garden soil and the other over a play area. Then place each string on a saucer of gelatin and replace the covers. Keep the third saucer of gelatin to act as a control. Set all aside in a cool place (Figure 34-3). What do you notice about these when you examine these in a few days' time? Make a report.

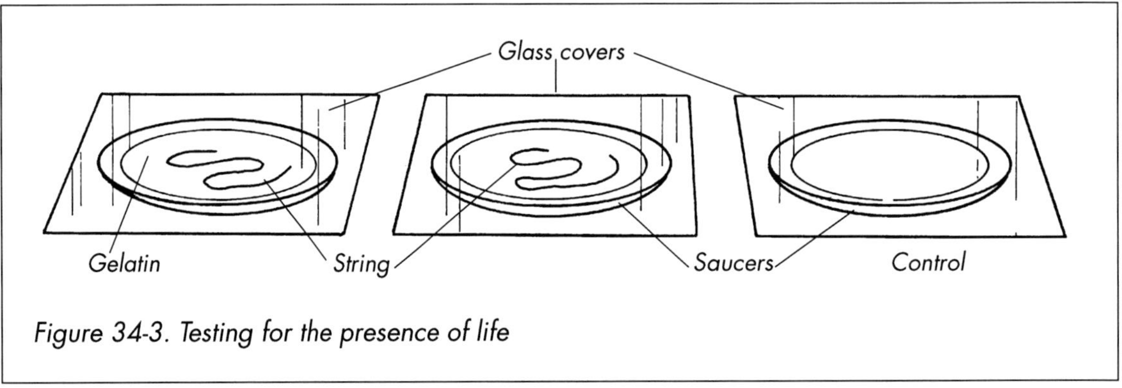

Figure 34-3. Testing for the presence of life

3. How might your experiments today be like those carried out by:

    a. astronomers searching for "wobbles"?

    b. a spacecraft searching for life-forms on another planet?

4. How did the *Viking* Lander on Mars search for life-forms?

CHAPTER FOUR

HUMANS IN SPACE

Medical Problems of Space Travel: The Physiology of Man in Space

Living things move around, breathe in air, take in food and water, excrete poisons and waste materials, grow, and reproduce other creatures like themselves. Living things also possess a nervous system. By means of receptor devices, we constantly receive information from the environment and respond or adjust ourselves in a particular way. "Irritability" describes this important property of living things.

Much of the information in the world around us can reach our awareness through our sensory organs—the ears, eyes, nose, tongue, and skin. These have been necessary for us to evolve to our present state. They make it possible for us to hear, see, smell, taste, and feel, and thereby add immeasurably to our appreciation of our environment.

Each sense organ responds only to a particular type of stimulus. Our eyes are light sensitive, our ears are sound sensitive. Sense buds in our tongue tell us that a food is sweet or bitter. Special cells in the nose pick up the fragrance of a flower or the acrid fumes of smoke. Our skin is the largest organ system. Covering the entire body, it protects against the outside world and enables us to adjust to the world as well. In contrast to the other organs, the skin responds to a variety of stimuli—heat, cold, pain, pressure, and touch.

All these sense organs require a sensory system that performs with a high degree of efficiency. The sensory system has three main parts: receptors, nerve pathways, and the brain, which is a kind of central arrival platform for incoming impulses. Sensations, feelings, and awareness result from the integrated activity of all of these.

The receptors of nerve endings react to various stimuli. The electrical messages from these stimuli pass along nerve fibers, enter the spinal cord, and travel along other fibers up to the higher centers of the brain. The brain interprets the messages as various types of sensation, depending on which receptors were stimulated.

Many internal parts of our bodies function independently of our will—heartbeat, gut movements, gland activity, size of the eye pupil, and so on, to name some examples. The sympathetic nervous system (not under direction of our will) monitors these. Our moods, feelings, and emotions play their part. A person blushes with shame or is white with anger, while fear produces a racing pulse and a dry mouth.

Space flight makes special demands on human emotional and nervous systems. Some of the stresses of concern to life scientists include:

a. radiation
b. heat or cold
c. vibration and noise
d. atmospheric gas content and pressure
e. acceleration
f. weightlessness
g. mental or psychological effects
h. how our eyes work on other worlds

Let us investigate these factors experimentally and look at their influence in our daily lives. Then consider the astronauts in the remote, hostile environment of space, confined in a spacecraft to the moon or Mars, isolated, lonely, far removed from the security of their earth home. How will the various stresses affect the space traveler? Will the stresses affect astronauts singly, or will they synergize (add together)? How will they influence a person's power of judgment, reasoning, decision-making ability, and skill in the manual control of the spacecraft on extended space flights?

35. Space Pilot Tests

Astronauts who act as pilots during space flight must be very skillful, reliable, and constantly aware of any dangers or risks during the period in orbit. They must be able at all times to carry out the tasks they have been trained to do, yet always remain calm and stable, not getting overly upset by mishaps. During the flight of *Apollo 13*, an oxygen tank in the service module exploded not long after takeoff. This deactivated most of the spacecraft's systems. Yet the astronauts completed the trip to the moon and back again, splashing down on earth safely. So in selecting astronauts, the psychological factor is extremely important. Before he or she is considered for the job of space pilot, an astronaut recruit undergoes tests designed to show up any physical shortcomings that would handicap him or her as the pilot of a spacecraft.

Could You Be an Astronaut?

You can find out how good you are at seeing in depth, in a field of vision test and in a hand steadiness test.

What you need: cardboard, tacks or drawing pins, wooden base made as shown, nails, two long pieces of string, slider (small piece of wood), aluminum or tin foil, flashlight bulb, holder, battery, wire, tape, tools, small metal screwdriver

1. Depth perception test:

    a. Cut eyeholes about 2 cm across and smaller string holes in one piece of cardboard as shown. Then fix the cardboard to the wood base with tacks or drawing pins. Drive a flathead nail into one side of the base about halfway along and the other into the wood slider. Place other drawing pins as shown. Thread the string through the holes and around the outer sides of the fixed nail and rear drawing pins, and tie the ends to the slider pins (Figure 35-1).

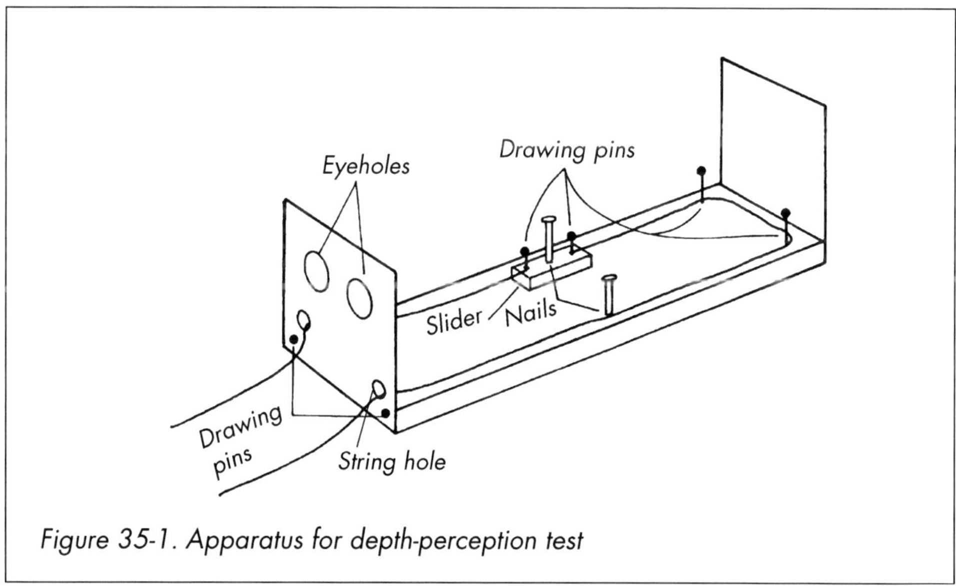

Figure 35-1. Apparatus for depth-perception test

    b. Move the sliding nail to different positions. How well are you able to judge the relative distance of objects in space? Can you line up the two nails exactly? Could you use your apparatus to judge the relative sizes of objects in space?

2. Field of vision test: Arrange the piece of shiny metal foil as shown. (If necessary use a cardboard backing.) Focus the eyes straight ahead. How far to the right or left can you see? Are both eyes just as good (Figure 35-2)?

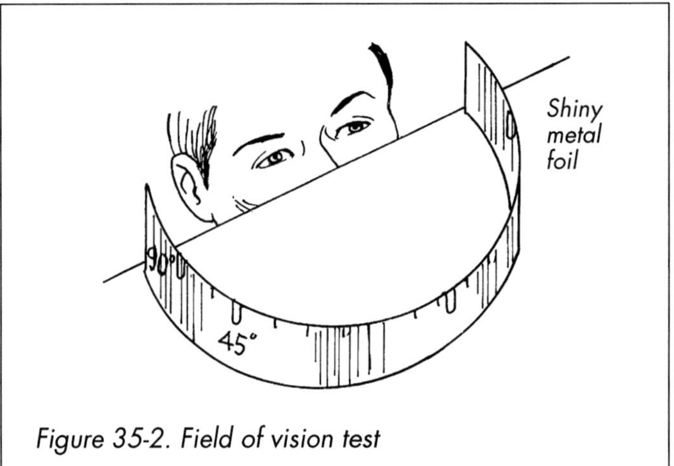

Figure 35-2. Field of vision test

3. Hand steadiness test: Hold the small metal screwdriver in a steady grip and move it along between the two pieces of bare copper wire as shown in Figure 35-3. How good is your hand control ability? How far can you move the screwdriver along without touching the wire and making the bulb flash?

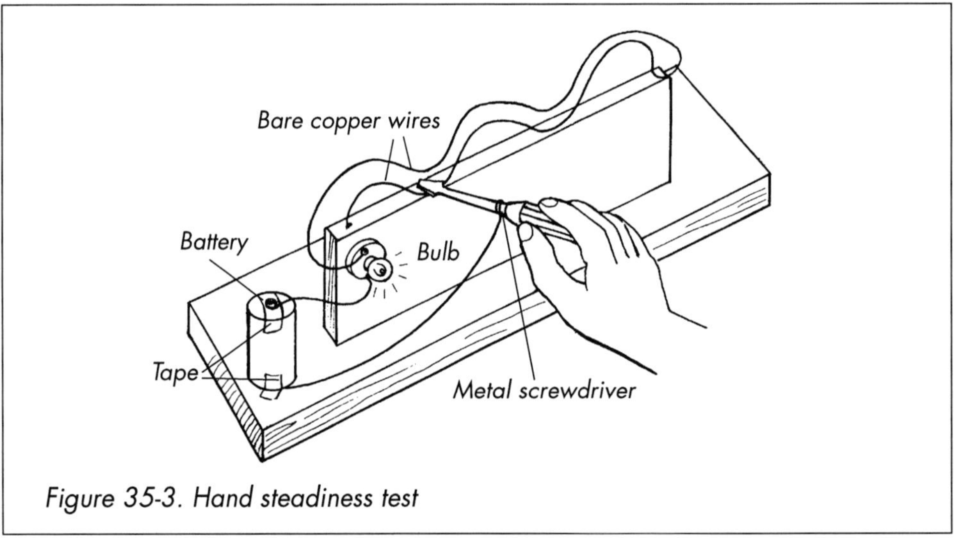

Figure 35-3. Hand steadiness test

36. Recycling in Space

Water is an essential part of our daily diet. It serves as the vehicle for countless chemical reactions within our bodies. It is also the vehicle by which body wastes and poisons are removed.

Water is lost from our bodies in our breath, through perspiration, and in excreta. Each of us produces more water than we take in, as the oxygen we breathe combines with hydrogen in our food to form extra water, H_2O.

Shower water and body water are two sources of water that may be reused after purification. In a spacecraft, such wastewater may be stored in collection tanks to which special chemicals are added to prevent the action of bacteria and the formation of gas. Evaporation and filtration are processes used to obtain pure water from impure.

In a future space station, water will be condensed out of cabin air, distilled from urine, and collected from hygiene activities. The water will then pass through a potable water processor. This complex of devices will first filter the water to remove particles, then heat it to kill microbes. The water will then pass through columns of activated charcoal and ion exchange resins, which remove hydrocarbons and metals. Organic compounds will be removed by a catalyst device, then iodine will be added and tests will be done for water quality.

A similar revitalization system for air is planned; a closed air loop can be added to the station later on.

Around the United States, scientists and contractors are working toward bio-regenerative systems that produce food as well as water. These will be useful on future space flights or in space colonies. See also Farming in Space, page 129.

Purifying Water

You can experiment with ways for purifying water.

What you need: water, ready-made powdered charcoal (or wood chips, tin lid, sand, spirit lamp), cold tea (or use a solution containing one drop of cochineal—red dye—to 1 tsp of water), filter funnel, cotton batting, small beaker, iodine solution, egg white

1. To make powdered charcoal, put some wood chips in a shallow tin and cover with about 3 cm of sand. Heat this over a spirit or gas flame for five minutes (you will need a strong flame) to convert the wood to charcoal (Figure 36-1).

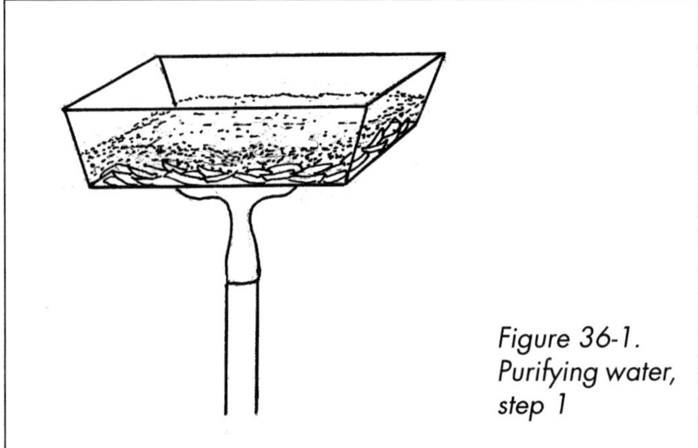

Figure 36-1. Purifying water, step 1

2. Place some powdered charcoal in the cold tea or cochineal solution. Shake the mixture for a few seconds, then filter it through a funnel containing some cotton batting (Figure 36-2). What is the color of the liquid that comes through, called the filtrate? How does the color compare with that of the original mixture? What has taken up the color?

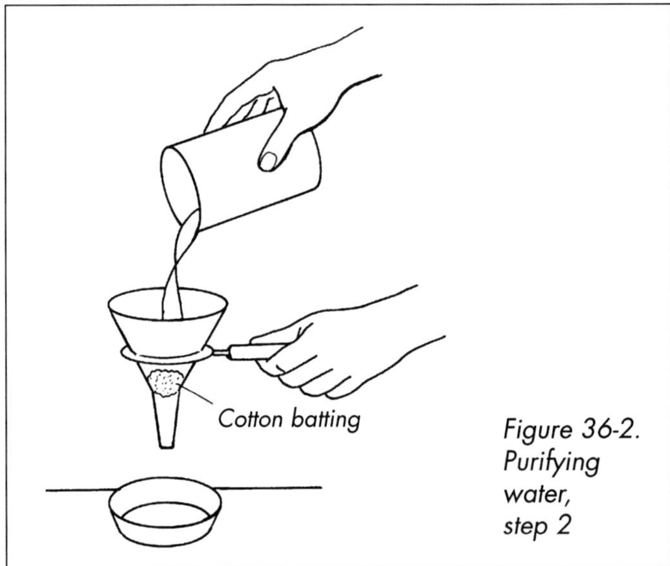

Figure 36-2. Purifying water, step 2

3. Water may contain bacteria that cause disease, but chemicals can be used to destroy these bacteria. Take a small beaker or glass half-filled with water and add six drops of iodine solution, making the water a pale brown color. Add 10 drops of egg white and allow the mixture to stand for 30 minutes. Does the egg white change in appearance? How? As egg white and bacteria bodies are both protein, what effect would you expect iodine to have on bacteria?

4. See if you can find out how your town water supply is filtered, and how disease-producing bacteria are eliminated from your drinking water.

37. Memory and Habit

Scientists know that a chemical called RNA, or ribonucleic acid, which is found in the nervous system, is made up of long chains of molecules that can rearrange themselves in many ways. Some scientists think that by means of these rearrangements, the nervous system can code and store information coming into the body.

Some data about RNA has come from experiments done on flatworms (planaria). These simple wormlike creatures can be trained to respond to a light and to run a simple maze. If a flatworm is cut in half, each half regroups. Flatworms also eat one another. When a trained flatworm is cut in half, each half passes onto the other half some of the original learning. An untrained worm eating a trained worm also remembers the training.

Other scientists doing the same experiments have not been able to get these results.

Does Practice Make Perfect?

You can study flatworms and find out how practice helps in learning.

What you need: flatworms, shallow bowl, pond water, piece of liver, hand lens, list of 10 four-digit numbers, fork, ball

1. Look in stagnant ponds or slow-moving water for flatworms, or buy them. Place a piece of liver in the shallow bowl of water and add some flatworms. Change the water regularly and observe the worms through the hand lens for a few weeks. If one worm is damaged, watch to see if each half grows a whole new worm. Can you build a maze and train a flatworm to find its way?

2. Try forming a habit by writing with the hand you don't usually use for that purpose. After a few days of repeated effort, can you use either hand more easily? Try this also when throwing a ball or holding a fork. Demonstrate the same idea by repeatedly trying to read an upside-down page.

3. Investigate how practice helps in learning. Have a friend prepare a list of four-digit numbers such as 1342, 6516, 5853, 9176, 1234, 3762, 5214, 2178, 6978, and 7531. Just before your friend reads the numbers to you, he tells you that you are to write each number backward. He allows you four seconds between numbers. After the test, he gives you a list of the correct answers and you mark yours. Now have a five-minute practice period with other numbers to improve your skill in writing numbers backward. Now try the original test again. What do you find? Have you improved because of the practice?

38. Artificial Gravity

Weightlessness, the state of seeming to have no weight, can be eliminated in a space station by creating an artificial gravity. So designers plan wheel-like space stations that will rotate. The slight rotating motion produces a sensation of gravity. The astronauts inside the space station will experience a sense of weight and will come to rest on the floor around the outside.

The world's largest artificial gravity simulator is at the Rockwell Company in the United States. It is built from an aircraft cabin and is mounted on a beam nearly 50 meters in diameter. The device is rather like a ride at a fair. During experimental test runs, four people ride the simulator at 4 rpm. After week-long rides, no discomfort is experienced.

Creating "Gravity" with Rotation

You can create artificial gravity by rotating objects.

What you need: pail of water, wooden coat hanger, coin, cardboard tube, bicycle, scissors, appropriate open area

1. Swing the pail of water through four or five circles. What happens to the water in the pail? Explain why. How is this an artificial gravity? What happens if you slow down the speed of swing?

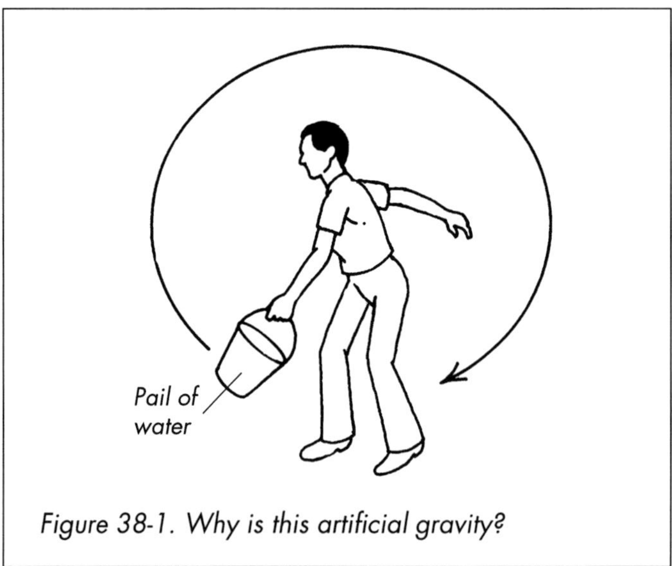

Figure 38-1. Why is this artificial gravity?

2. Place the coin on the coat hanger as shown in Figure 38-2. Swing it around on your first finger. What happens? Explain how the earth's gravity pull is overcome.

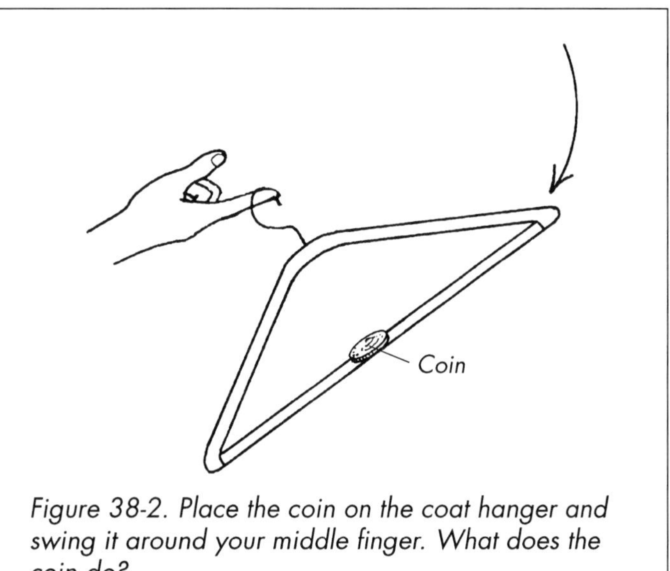

Figure 38-2. Place the coin on the coat hanger and swing it around your middle finger. What does the coin do?

3. Cut the cardboard tube along one side and slip it over one of the spokes of the bicycle wheel. Set the wheel spinning. What happens? What forces are at work?

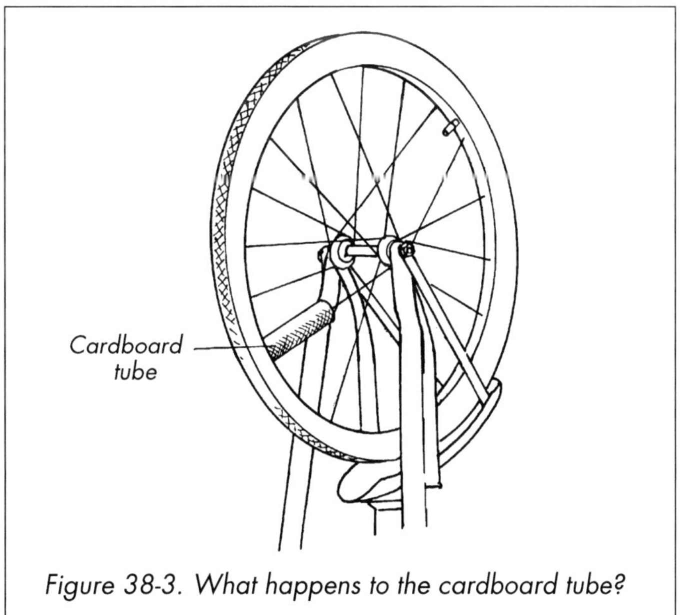

Figure 38-3. What happens to the cardboard tube?

4. Write a paragraph telling how your experiments have helped you to understand what artificial gravity is. How will it be achieved in a space station high above the earth?

5. Out in space, far away from the gravity pull of the planets, objects are weightless. People in space become a little taller. Find out why.

39. Seeing in Space and on Other Worlds

Space travelers will have to cope with very bright and very dim light when traveling in space. Astronauts eventually exploring other worlds may also meet the same extremes of light. Their eyes (and animal eyes) adjust automatically to the changes in light strengths we all meet during each day. But for intense brightness and black landscapes, light filters and electronic aids will have to be used to help explorers to see.

Photo 13. Astronaut James S. Voss encounters changes in light and dark as he "walks" in space around the space shuttle Endeavor. *Can you see the* Endeavor's *front section reflected in Voss's visor?*

Parts of our eyes act to protect our sight; other parts receive and record what we see. The clear outer part of the eye, the cornea, is a cover for the colored part of the eye, the iris, and the round dark circle in the center, the pupil (see Figure 39-1). Just as a car has built-in windshield washers, so also our eyes have tear glands that wash away dust or foreign matter that blows into them. And further, just as some cars have headlight covers, so our eyes have eyelids that can instantly cover the eye or open it up.

The colored part of the eye, the iris, is muscle. Like all our muscles, it can relax or contract. So the iris, as in a camera, controls the amount of light that enters the eye by setting the size of the pupil, big or tiny, at the center. The eye lens, like a camera lens, focuses the light rays on the light-sensitive part of the eye, the retina. The retina is a kind of film, sensitive to all the shades of light. Leaving the back of the eye is the large optic nerve, which carries the messages of light to the brain. The brain interprets the messages for us.

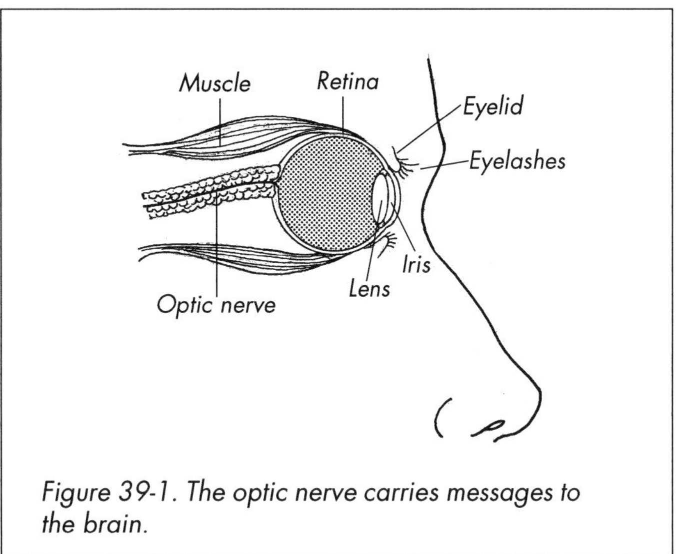

Figure 39-1. The optic nerve carries messages to the brain.

Seeing in the Light and in the Dark

You can test how your eyes react to bright and dim light.

What you need: mirror, paper, book, electric lamp, pieces of colored cellophane

1. To see how the size of your pupils is affected by dark and light, close your eyes and cover them with your hands for a couple of minutes. Then hold the mirror in front of your eyes and open them. What do you note about the pupils? How does this affect the amount of light entering the eye? How does the iris do this? How is it done in your camera?

2. Roll several sheets of paper into a hollow tube. Place this on the print of a book so that you are trying to read in the dark. How long is it before you can see the print? Now look quickly into the mirror. Do you see the pupils of your eyes closing in the brighter light (Figure 39-2)?

Figure 39-2. Test of eye reaction to bright and dim light

3. With the use of filters of various colors and thicknesses, the pupil will keep its usual size no matter how bright the light. Turn on an electric lamp and look at the bright bulb through the pieces of colored cellophane. Can you read the words on the bulb? Combine the pieces in various ways. Which combinations and thicknesses make for the easiest reading (Figure 39-3)?

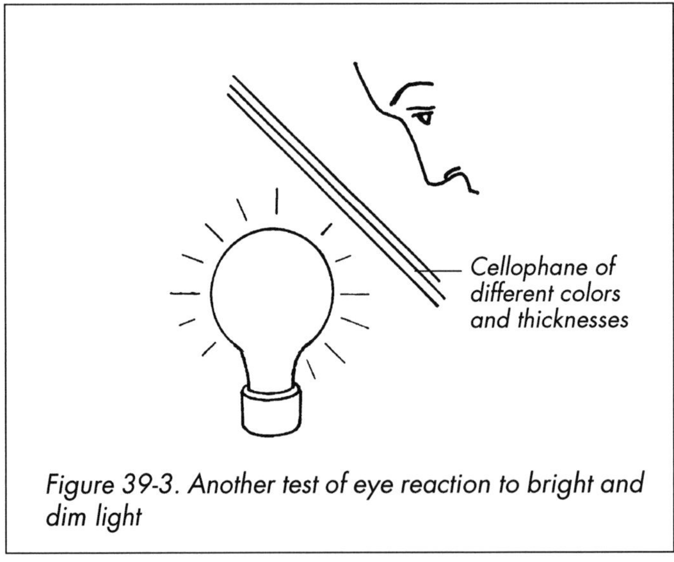

Figure 39-3. Another test of eye reaction to bright and dim light

4. Outdoor observations for class groups or students at home: Look at the pupils of a cat's, sheep's or lizard's eyes in dim light. Are they opened more widely than in bright daylight? Find out whether fowl see well in the dark. When do they go to roost? Owls can see in the dark. Find out how and why.

40. Space Suit Air-Conditioning

> *Then felt I like a watcher of the skies*
> *When a new planet swims into his ken . . .*
>
> —John Keats

Space suits are an important part of the space shuttle *Orbiter* equipment. They are carried on every mission and make it possible for astronauts to leave the spacecraft for emergency work outside, repairs to satellites during space walks, and so on. Space suits worn by *Apollo* astronauts protected the wearers and allowed lunar exploration and the setting up of scientific experiments on the moon's surface.

A space suit has to provide all the supplies the astronaut needs when leaving the protective cabin of the spacecraft—water, oxygen, heat, radio communication, and waste disposal for up to seven hours. The underwear part of the suit has 80 meters of tubing that carries cooling water. There is also a device to collect urine. The leg part of the suit has boots attached and is pulled on. The upper part of the suit is rigid fiberglass and is attached by the backpack to the inner wall of the shuttle air lock. The wearer slides upward into this. The Portable Life Support Systems (PLSS) unit carries consumables, emergency oxygen, and controls mounted on a smaller chest pack.

Air conditioning units keep the airtight pressure suits from becoming uncomfortable. Dry, temperature-adjusted air that circulates through the inside of the suit removes moisture and helps cool the astronaut's body. When the astronaut is in the spacecraft, the main life-support system performs these functions.

The head-gear or "Snoopy" cap carries microphones. The gloves (15 sizes are available) are secured in place by aluminum ring fittings. The helmet of polycarbonate with its covers and visors comes last. The suit weighs 38.5 kg and protects the astronaut against temperatures in space, the vacuum, and micrometeoroid particles. As two astronauts always go out together, there is backup should an emergency arise. Before venturing out, the astronauts breathe pure oxygen at the suit's pressure, roughly one third of cabin pressure, for $3\frac{1}{2}$ hours. The astronauts make their exit from the shuttle via a cylindrical air lock and so arrive in the bottom of the payload bay.

Experiments with Air and Temperature

You can demonstrate some properties of air and some aspects of temperature control.

What you need: bottle, salt, tablespoon, glass of soil, square of cardboard, piece of cloth, two thermometers, dish of water, card, fan or hair drier, piece of tubing

1. Run some water from the tap into a bottle and stand it on the window sill. What causes the bubbles to form? What are the bubbles? Where have they come from? When the air bubbles have stopped rising, pour a tablespoon of salt into the bottle and shake. Does this bring more bubbles out of the water?

2. Warm some water in the sun or heat it in some other way. Does this bring bubbles out of the water? Why should you keep an aquarium in a cool place?

3. Run some water into the glass of soil until it covers the soil level. Do you see bubbles of air rising? What living things in the soil require air? How does a farmer or gardener make sure air gets into the soil?

4. Put some lukewarm water on the back of your hand. Help it to evaporate by waving a card back and forth. What do you notice? Can you explain the cooling effect?

5. Use thread to fix a corner of the cloth to the bulb of a thermometer. Place the other end of the cloth in a dish of water. After a few minutes, water will seep through the cloth and around the bulb of the thermometer. Have another thermometer alongside (keep it dry); fan both with the hair drier or by waving a card energetically. After a few minutes take the readings of both thermometers. Explain why they are different. A small difference in temperature means greater or lesser humidity (Figure 40-1).

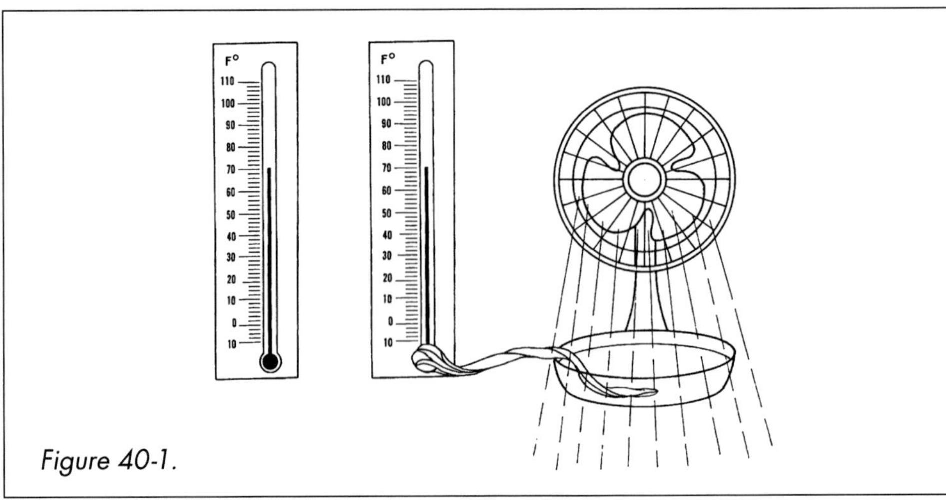

Figure 40-1.

6. Fill a glass to overflowing with water and place a piece of cardboard over the mouth. Turn the glass upside down gently, keeping the cardboard in place as you do so. Take your hand from the cardboard. What keeps the water in the glass? Now place the inverted glass in a soup plate of water and slide the card away. What keeps the glass full now? Pass a piece of tubing through the water to the top of the glass. Blow into it. What happens? Why? Now suck. What happens? Why (Figure 40-2)?

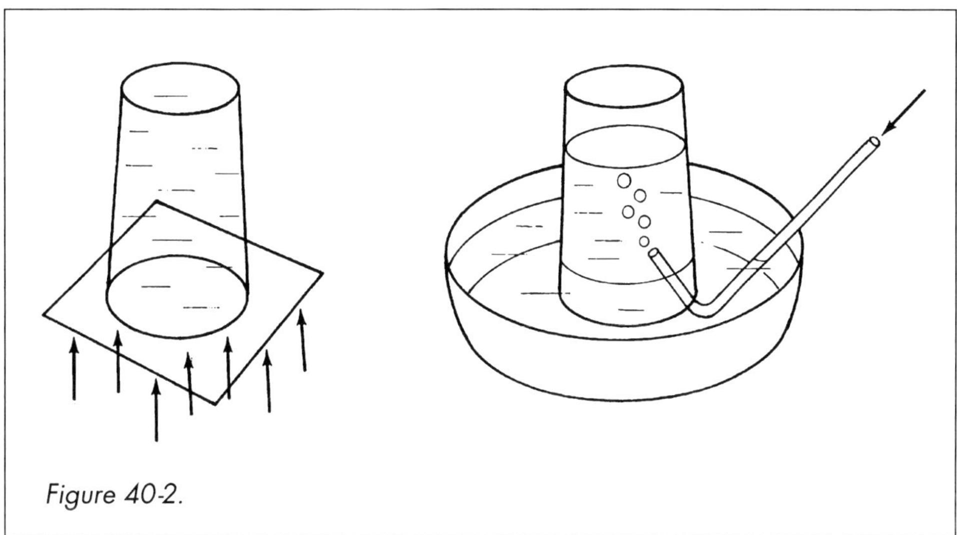

Figure 40-2.

41. Farming in Space

> *Ah, but a man's reach should exceed his grasp,*
> *Or what's a heaven for?*
>
> —Robert Browning

A space station is a huge orbiting structure with large living and working quarters. It can be manned part-time or permanently. Early space stations included the Russian *Soyuz* and *Salyut* in 1970 and the American *Skylab*. Then in the 1980's the space shuttle began the Space-Lab program. The next stage will be to build space stations in orbit. The United States, with participation from other countries, plans to build a space station sometime in the near future. It will probably be 110 m (500 ft) long and have great sail-like panels for capturing solar energy. It will also have living quarters, a laboratory, manufacturing areas, storage, a control center, and dock facilities for space shuttles. It will orbit the earth at a height of 300 km (185 miles).

As astronauts stay longer in space, the need for a well-balanced and more varied diet becomes greater. In current experiments, plant seedlings are grown in trays. One tray may be upside down. Below it, another tray may be right side up, with a fluorescent light source acting as sun in between. Even without gravity, the roots grow to a nutrient (a mixture of chemicals), and the leaves grow toward the light source. The mercury vapor of a fluorescent light is dangerous to take into space, so there is a need for an alternative artificial sun. It is possible that light-emitting-diodes (L.E.D.), the same as those found in TV remote controls, will be the choice.

Sowing seeds in space is not a matter of "plow and scatter" as on the earth. Special containers called cassettes are used—one seed per cassette for germination. Healthy seedlings are placed in cassettes and then transferred to salad trays to grow. In weightlessness, putting water where the roots are is not the best way to go about it. The water floats around, mixes up with air, and does not necessarily go where the roots are. So a special membrane that contains water is used. The roots can wrap around this membrane and absorb water and nutrients from its semipermeable walls. Lettuces, carrots, and radishes are crops from the salad machine. For a crew of four, there would be three salads per person per week.

Growing Plants Without Soil

You can experiment with soilless gardening, the growing of plants by chemical solutions (hydroponics).

What you need: packets of seeds (carrot, sweet pepper, lettuce, petunia, tomato), trough or pots, tap water, washed sand or potting soil, 26 g calcium nitrate, 8.5 g potassium acid phosphate (KH_2PO_4), 18.5 g magnesium sulphate, 2.5 g ferrous sulphate, glass jars with plastic tops, metric measure, stirrer, pH indicator, wooden or plastic spatula, paper, tube with bulb (e.g., atomizer), cotton batting or muslin

1. Plant your seeds in a trough or pot. Fill with sand or potting soil to within 3 cm of the top, then place 10–12 tomato seeds, spaced 2–3 cm apart, over the growing medium. Cover the seeds with about $\frac{1}{2}$–1 cm of the medium. Moisten well with tap water. Be sure to keep the medium moist but not soggy. Overwatering can lead to plant death, as not enough oxygen may get through. As the young seedlings grow, be certain they get plenty of sunlight. The plant seeds contain enough food supply for the first growth of plants. The chemical nutrients are not used until the young plant is about 3 cm tall and has its first true leaves. Sow some other seeds (e.g., lettuce) in another container in the same way.

2. The chemicals above are sufficient to make up 35–36 liters of solution. To make your solutions, use glass or porcelain containers, not metals. Metal may react and spoil your preparation.

    Dissolve the calcium nitrate in 600 ml (two cupfuls) of water in a suitable storage jar. Then in separate jars, dissolve the magnesium sulphate and the potassium acid phosphate, using 300 ml of water for each jar. Label each jar with the name of the chemical. These stock solutions you have made should be diluted before use. To make $4\frac{1}{2}$ liters (or 1 gallon) of solution, use the metric measure to place $4\frac{1}{2}$ liters of water in a large container, then add to this from the stock solutions in the order stated: 35 ml ($\frac{1}{8}$ cup) magnesium sulphate, 35 ml ($\frac{1}{8}$ cup) potassium acid phosphate. Stir well. Then add 75 ml ($\frac{1}{4}$ cup) calcium nitrate and stir. Added together in this way, the potassium acid phosphate helps prevent precipitation of the insoluble calcium sulphate. If you wish to make smaller quantities of solutions, use smaller quantities of water and chemicals in proportion.

    Just prior to using your mixed nutrients, add a pinch of ferrous sulphate and stir to dissolve. You add the ferrous sulphate in this way because it oxidizes and precipitates in the presence of phosphate.

3. Use the pH paper to check the acidity of your nutrient mix. Water, which is neutral, has a pH of 7. Solutions with a pH less than 7 are acid. If the pH is greater than 7, the solution is alkaline. Because most plants thrive in a slightly acid environment, it is important that your preparation has a slightly acid pH, between 5 and 6.8. Cut a 1.5-cm piece of the indicator paper and test the acidity of the mixed nutrient. What color do you get? Is it on the acid side of the pH?

4. Transfer the seedlings to a wide-mouth jar with a plastic top. Cover the jar with metal foil or opaque paper to keep the light out. Otherwise, green algae and other small water plants will grow in the nutrient. By using up oxygen, these tiny plants will interfere with the growth of your seedlings.

    Pour the mixed nutrient into the jar to within 1–2 cm of the top. In the plastic top of the jar, cut several holes 1 cm in diameter. Support your seedling in this with a small piece of cotton batting or muslin (Figure 41-1).

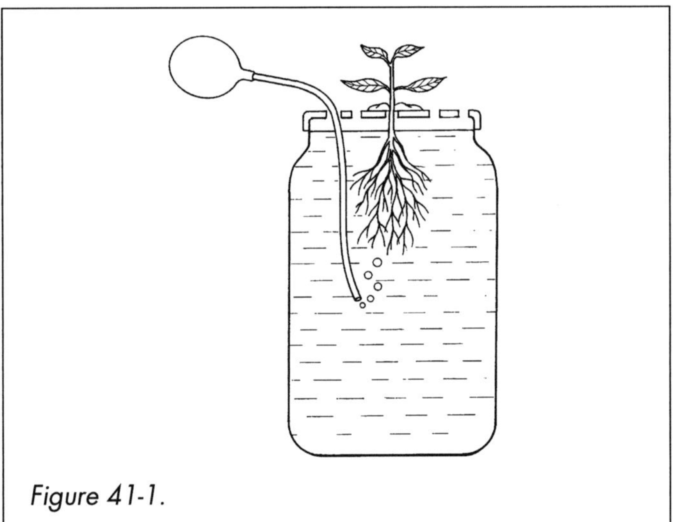

Figure 41-1.

5. Remove your plant from the sand, using a wooden or plastic spatula to loosen the sand around the roots. Be gentle to avoid any damage to the roots. Hold the seedling lightly with your fingers and lift it out with the aid of the spatula. Then transfer it to the jar, making certain the roots reach down into the solution. Oxygen needs to be present for the absorption of minerals, so the plant roots must have air. The air space between the lid and the liquid level helps supply this. Make sure this space is about 5 cm.

    The solution must be aerated at least once a day. To do this, use the bulb and tube. Have the free end of the tube in the solution ,and press the bulb to blow air through the solution. A bulb from an atomizer is specially suitable for this.

6. For best results, change the nutrient about once a week. This ensures that sufficient elements are present all the time. The easiest way is to add nutrient to another jar, then transfer the plant—support and all—to the new jar in one movement. Throw out the old solution. As with all growing plants, be sure your seedlings receive plenty of sunshine and warmth.

    As your plants grow, you will need to give them support. A string hanging from a hook in the ceiling, with the other end tied loosely around the base of the young plant, would be as easy to make as any.

7. Repeat the above steps for the other kinds of seeds. Compare plants grown in nutrient solutions with those grown in soil in similar environmental conditions. Do you find any differences? Would the method you have used above for growing plants be suitable for farming in space, or would it need to be modified? If so, how?

8. Make a display of your plants grown with chemical nutrients. Add labels that explain what you have done.

42. Vibration and Noise

French scientists carrying out research on low frequency vibrations (infrasound) have shown that these impair human concentration and efficiency. They also produce a sense of sickness. Breathing, heart action, hearing, and even mental balance seem to be affected. An accidental blast was reported to have produced paralysis in one member of a research team.

Of special interest to NASA was the effect of such vibrations on ground staff during the testing of *Saturn* rockets. The French team, studying noises in their suburb, found that an air compressor gave vibrations near the danger frequency of seven cycles per second.

Seeing Sound

You can see what sound vibrations look like by making a sound vibration detector.

What you need: one medium-size fruit can with both ends cut out, balloon rubber, rubber bands, a small chip of mirror about $\frac{1}{2}$ cm square, adhesive

1. Stretch the piece of balloon rubber over one end of the tin can and fix it there with a rubber band. Put tape around the other rim to avoid getting cut.

2. Stick the tiny piece of mirror to the balloon rubber at about one third the diameter from the edge (Figure 42-1).

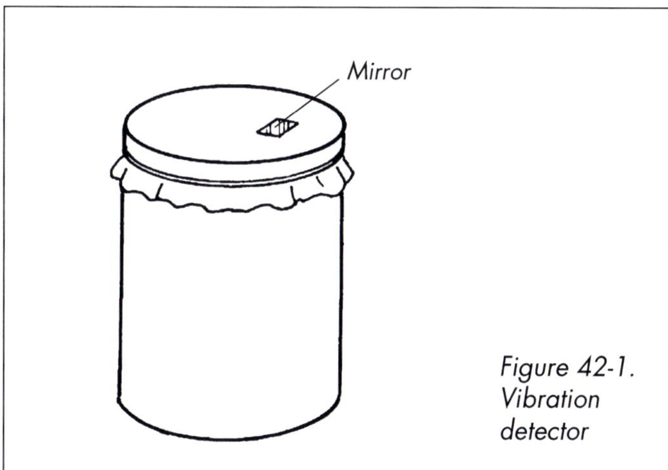

Figure 42-1. Vibration detector

3. Sit in strong sunlight and reflect a beam of sunlight to make a spot on the wall or ceiling.

4. Press the open end of the can against your mouth and sing different notes into the can (Figure 42-2). What do you see the spot of light doing? How many different patterns can you get? Try a soft note, then the same note loud. Does the pattern vary? Describe how. Try the effect of high- and low-pitched sounds on the patterns you see. Do the sounds give different patterns?

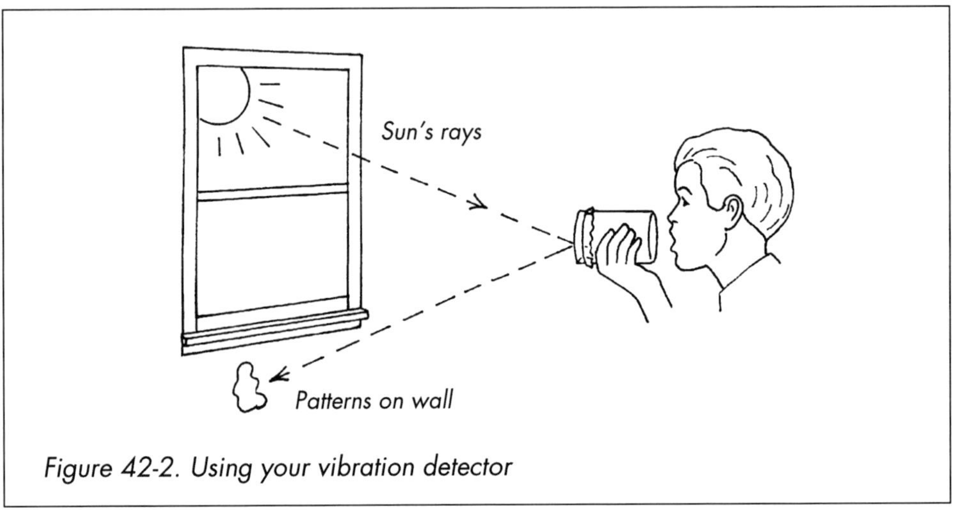

Figure 42-2. Using your vibration detector

5. Try holding a small transistor radio against the mouth of the can. What differences do you note as the volume is increased?

43. Acceleration

A space traveler is exposed to forces of acceleration at launch, during insertion into orbit, and again during reentry. These forces show in the soft supporting tissues, the bony tissues, various body organs, and body fluids.

The effects vary depending on the magnitude, direction, and duration of the force applied. Accelerations across the body up to 6 g produce a sensation of increased pressure. Between 6 and 8 g breathing becomes difficult. Blood pressure may be reduced to such a level that disturbances in vision and consciousness may occur.

Studying the Effects of Acceleration

You can demonstrate the effect of acceleration on a body.

What you need: metal ball or other small, heavy object such as a lead sinker, clear plastic jar, strand of rubber (as from rubber band or golf ball), pencil

1. Suspend the rubber ball or other small, heavy object by a single strand of rubber in the jar. At rest, the pull of the rubber matches the weight of the ball.

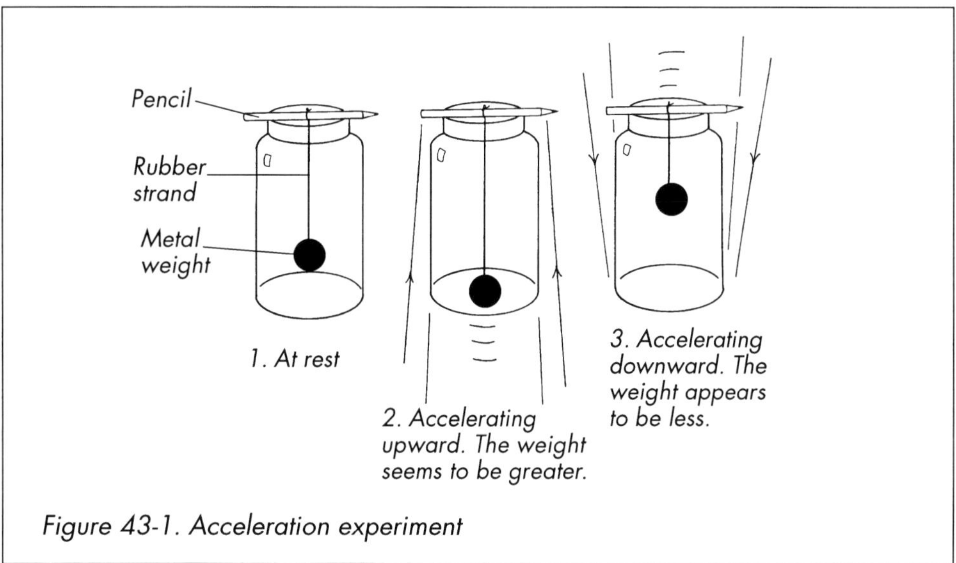

Figure 43-1. Acceleration experiment

2. Now, holding the jar, accelerate it upward as far as you can stretch. What do you note about the length of the rubber as you do this? How is the ball acting—as if its weight had increased?

3. Next, accelerate the jar downward. How does the ball behave? What does this suggest about its weight?

4. Can you relate these observations to astronauts in the space shuttle as it lifts off the launch pad and accelerates away into orbit? What happens in the same space shuttle during return to earth (reentry)?

44. Exploring Mars

> *Yesterday is already a dream; tomorrow is still a vision.*
> *Today well-lived makes yesterday a dream of happiness,*
> *tomorrow a vision of hope.*
>
> —Ancient Sanskrit proverb

The spacecraft *Pathfinder* was scheduled to be launched in 1996 and land on Mars in July 1997. Instead of using a rocket engine to slow it down to orbital speed, *Pathfinder* would aerobrake right into the Martian atmosphere, deploy a parachute at 10 km altitude, and within 100 m of the surface, fire small rockets to arrest its descent. After landing, three "petals" would open to stabilize the lander. During its first day on the surface, *Pathfinder* would beam to Earth pictures of its surroundings.

On the next day a small, independent, robotic rover would roll out and perform experiments on the rocks and soil. Once planned to be the size of a jeep, the prototype rover is now the size of a toy truck. The full-scale model weighs 22 pounds; you could pick it up with your two hands. This is all made possible by microelectronics.

The new Mars rover has six independently articulated wheels. If the front pair go over a cliff, the rest automatically go into reverse and pull the craft back. The rover can navigate around obstacles and can scoop up samples of the Martian soil and analyze them for chemical makeup. Other onboard equipment includes a drill that can bore into rock centers. The rover will also deploy an alpha-proton-X ray spectrometer (APXS) to scan Martian rocks.

The micro-rover aims to discover how such a vehicle will perform on Mars' little-understood surface. Then future rovers with different missions would be better designed to move about and perform experiments. The U.S. *Mariner* space probes *4, 6,* and *9* showed Mars as a well-cratered world very like our arid, lifeless moon. Then the two *Vikings*, which touched down on Mars in 1976, searched for life and found none. With no protective ozone layer, ultraviolet radiation relentlessly sterilizes the surface of Mars.

This brings up questions: How did Mars come to its present frigid, apparently sterile, and very thin atmospheric state? Could life have begun long ago on a warmer, wetter Mars and can a fossil record be found? What is there about Mars' history that may be relevant to planet Earth?

Photo 14. A mosaic of the planet Mars, composed of images taken by the 102 Viking Orbiter. In the center of the mosaic is the Valles Marineris canyon system, which is over 2,000 kilometers long and up to 8 kilometers deep. That is more than 5 times as long and almost 5 times as deep as the Grand Canyon.

Why Earth should teem with life while Mars appears to be a dead world is a question posed by Dr. Christopher McKay of NASA's Ames Research Center near San Francisco. He is in charge of the Mars rover project.

McKay has shown that about 4.5 billion years ago, not long after the solar system formed, both planets had lush atmospheres. But in each case gases were absorbed by surface rocks. On Earth, simple one-cell life forms lived on unaffected. Dr. McKay states that drastic surface movements on earth crushed these rocks, heating them up strongly. In volcanic eruptions the gases vented back to the atmosphere.

On Mars, by contrast, this did not take place. And because of gases being absorbed by the rocks, the atmosphere thinned away almost to nothing. At such low air pressure, water disappeared as a liquid. Since water is needed by all living cells, any life probably disappeared from the planet. But for the first one and a half billion years of Mars' babyhood, it is very likely there was life just as on Earth at the same time.

Where will a probe eventually go looking for life on Mars? Malcolm Walter of Macquarie University in Sydney, Australia, has been working with NASA scientists. The place to go, says Walter, is where there used to be hot springs! At hot springs sites on Earth such as Rotorua, New Zealand, or Yellowstone in Montana, there is rapid precipitation of minerals such as silica (sand) and calcium carbonate (lime). Walter found beautifully preserved fossil bacteria in 300-million-year-old quartz (a form of silica) from central Queensland, Australia. Other fossil bacteria have been found near hot springs in Nevada and Montana.

"If there was water on Mars (which we think there was) and there was a heat source (there must have been because we can see the old volcanoes), then there must have been hot springs," says Walter. "It's inescapable—you put water and heat together and you get hot springs."

Michael Carr of the U.S. Geological Survey adds, "If Mars did have a different climate—a warm, wet, hospitable climate—in the past, then the chances for life are considerably enhanced."

Exploring Mars on Your Own

You can make a model of the surface of Mars, try some chemical tests, and make a Mars rover.

What you need: large tray (about 30 × 45 cm) with raised edge or a deep-sided pan, cardboard, modeling clay or plaster of Paris, sand, red iron oxide, dilute hydrochloric acid, ammonium or potassium thiocyanate solution, candle, penknife, pencil, empty thread spools, drawing pins, file, marble or ball bearings, matches, pencils, sharp knife, protractor, rubber bands, string, watch with sweep second hand, books, pebbles

1. Cut cardboard to fit on the bottom of your tray. Use modeling clay or plaster of Paris to make models of mountains, volcano, craters, valleys, polar icecap, steep slopes, and gentle slopes as a model landscape of Mars. (Look at photos or drawings of Mars for ideas.) Add pebbles for a bouldered area and have a lake basin to represent Parana Valles.

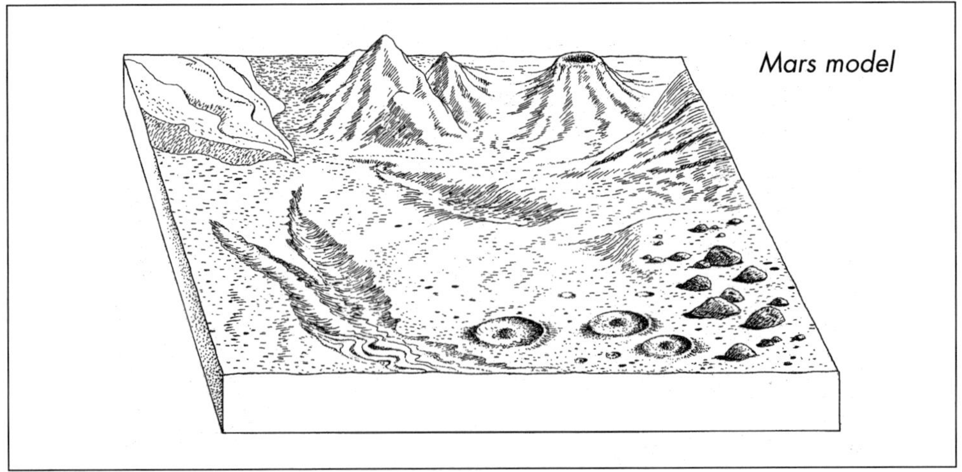

2. Add red oxide of iron to sand and mix it up so that the sand has a reddish color. When the plaster is dry, add this freely over the tray. This now represents the surface features of the Red Planet.

3. Test for iron in the "Martian soil" by taking a little of the sand and warming it up with a little dilute hydrochloric acid. This takes up any iron present to form iron chloride. To this solution, add a drop of thiocyanate solution. A red color is positive for iron.* What color do you get?

4. The Mars micro-rover will move around to study the planet's surface. Could you design one using a thread spool? Cut a 1 cm-thick slice of candle. Remove the wick by burning or cut it out with a sharp penknife.

5. Now assemble your Mars rover as in the sketch. With the first finger, turn the pencil around 20–30 times to twist the band and load it with energy (Figure 44-1). Test your rover on your desktop. How well does it perform? Would it perform as well on the surface of Mars? Could you improve its performance?

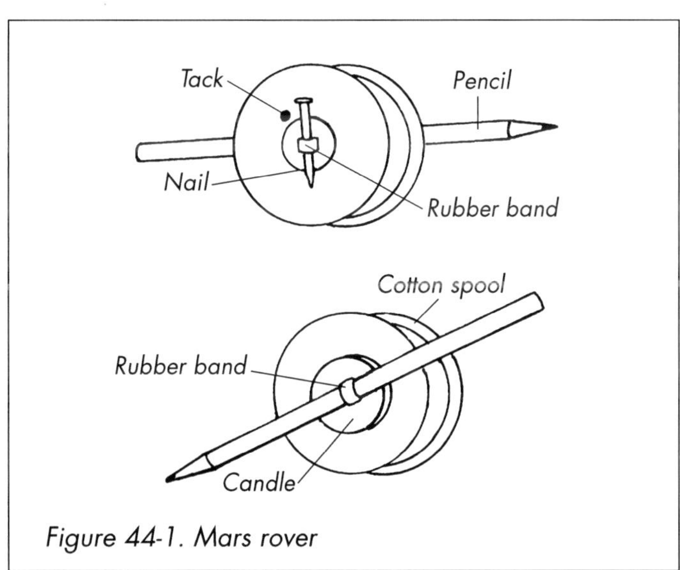

Figure 44-1. Mars rover

6. Use a file or sharp knife to make notches or teeth around the edges of the spool. Would the modified rover perform better on the surface of Mars? To find out, experiment with your rover on different parts of your Mars model. Or try it outside on rough terrain. How well does it perform? How does it compare with a rover that is not modified? How are the teeth helping (Figure 44-2)?

---

*A solution of an iron salt with thiocyanate gives a blood-red color. This is due to the iron thiocyanate that forms.

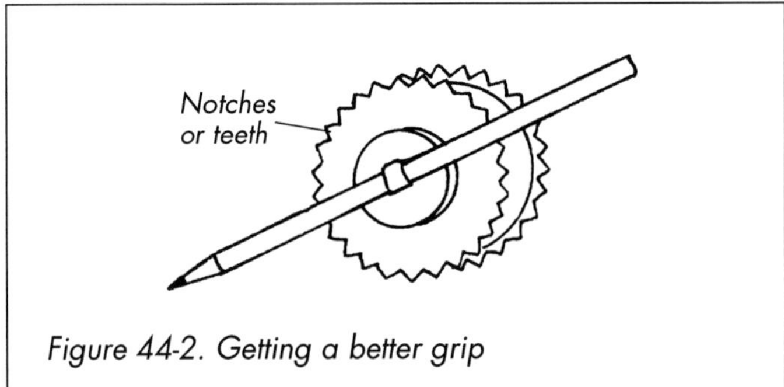

Figure 44-2. Getting a better grip

7. Climbing a crater wall or volcanic cone on Mars: What is the steepest slope your
   rover should attempt? Use your desktop to act as a crater wall: Fix the angle with
   a protractor and use a book as a wedge (Figure 44-3). Try 5°, 10°, 15°, 20°. Wind
   up your rover a set number of turns and use the same number for each of your
   attempts. Measure the time taken to climb the "crater wall" and record this on the
   graph (Figure 44-4). At what slope does your rover fail to make it?

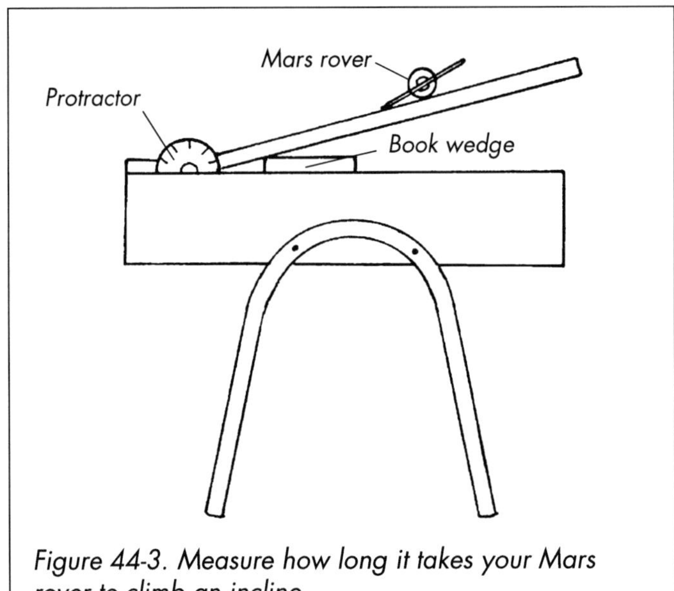

Figure 44-3. Measure how long it takes your Mars
rover to climb an incline.

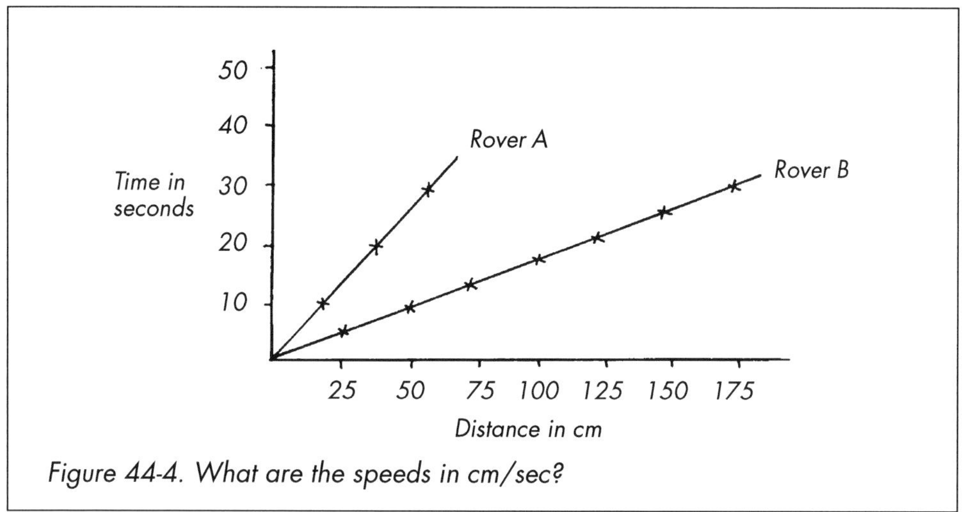

Figure 44-4. What are the speeds in cm/sec?

8. Design a twin-motor tractor or four-wheel-drive rover. Does its performance better match the conditions on Mars (Figure 44-5)?

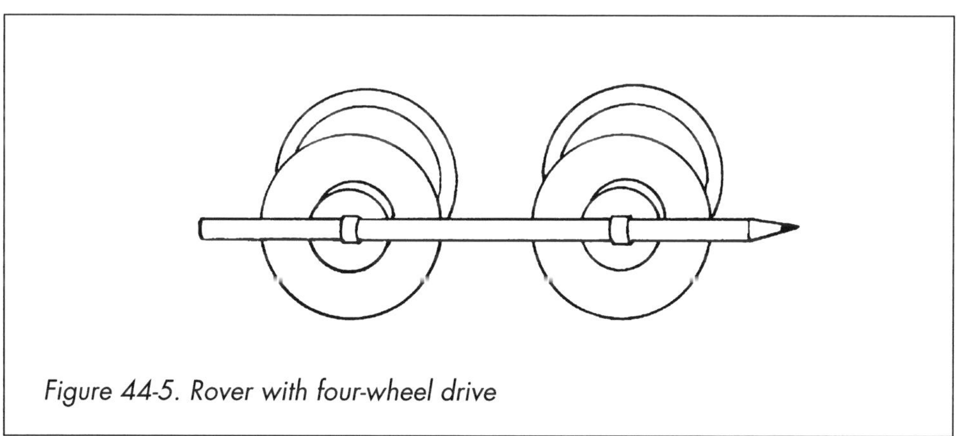

Figure 44-5. Rover with four-wheel drive

9. Use your Mars model for a display and show your rovers in action on it. Display also your graphs, and some pictures of Mars and the *Viking* Landers.

10. Stage a play about the first astronauts to land on Mars, with scenery based on your study of Mars.

INDEX